Golden Years

The Irish Guide to Planning Your Finances for Retirement

Declan Lyons

LIB
ERT
IES

Contents

1

Why This Book?

Most of us hope to retire; some of us look forward to that time with great enthusiasm. There is plenty of advice around about the financial products available, but few take account of the human dimension. We are all different; with our own dreams, desires and fears. We need to personalise our finances – particularly for our later years – to match these needs and desires.

This book draws its inspiration as much from my personal experience as my years working in and writing about personal finance and related business matters. A close relative died at the relatively young age of fifty-eight. He was a man with abundant enthusiasm for life and lived it to the full. He had great plans for his retirement; but sadly was never able to fulfil them. I've often wondered if he should have put some of these plans into action earlier and got some enjoyment from them – if only a small amount. These musings have inspired my own and my wife's retirement planning.

My own mother is still alive at ninety-one years of

11

age, but in need of constant nursing care. I've seen how few services are available for the elderly and how little the state does to care for them when they need it most. As a family, we have been fortunate to be able to afford the care that she needs and hopefully will be able to continue to do so into the future.

These two contrasting examples show the difficulties of planning for our personal futures. How much should we postpone now to ensure we have enough to provide for an uncertain number of years in the future? On the other hand, if we do put off until later what perhaps we could do now, are we risking never having the opportunity to enjoy those experiences?

This book guides you through the process of planning for your retirement. It will help you to work out how much you will need and how you can source these funds. It examines the different options open to you and explores how you can maximise your potential benefits. You won't find hard and fast rules because there aren't any – everybody is different, with very different needs and expectations. What this guide aims to do is help you to plan for the future that *you* want.

These are personal decisions and you'll find little to help you make them in the dry statistics of an actuary's tables. No, they are personal choices that should be informed by good financial information but not driven by it. What is important though is that, as much as possible, we ensure that we make the choices for ourselves and that we put the means in place to allow us to do so. This book sets out to help you build up and maintain the financial independence that you'll need to gain maximum control over your later life and the decisions that you make.

Golden years: When are they?

Our golden years are those in the latter part of our lives. They come after a lifetime of work and activity and should be a time when we can relax and enjoy ourselves. Most of us will have fewer responsibilities when we reach this stage in life: our children are reared and are now living independently; we will probably have paid for our home and most of its furnishings, and our income may have increased over the years leading up to our retirement. We want to have the financial wherewithal to enjoy this time fully. This guide looks at how you can plan and organise your finances so that you can.

The state has set sixty-five as the retirement age for most civil and public servants (you qualify for the non-contributory pension at sixty-six years of age). It used to be the case that most people retired at this age and then lived on a pension for their remaining years. Based on Central Statistics Office figures for 2006, at sixty-five, the average man can expect to live to 81.6 years (a further 16.6 years) while the average woman can expect to reach close to eighty-five years (a further 19.8 years). It's worth noting that, if you reach the age of seventy-five, then a man can expect to live close to the age of eighty-five, while a woman can reach eighty-seven.

We need to provide financially for these later years. This guide's underlying philosophy aims to help people have sufficient funds to enjoy their retirement to the maximum – rather than maximise their funds. In other words, this guide is about having money to spend rather than squirreling it away for your heirs.

It also recognises that providing for your retirement has to be done in the context of living in the present. There is little point in living in deprivation now so that you can live more comfortably later. You need to strike a balance between present and future comfort.

I've used the subtitle 'planning your finances for retirement'. But retirement isn't what it used to be. Things have become more complicated. Some people want to retire earlier; others plan to continue working in some way long after their official retirement date. Others may wish to make a complete change in their lives in their later years. Pensions, savings and investment products have become more complicated, too. This guide will help you to negotiate this complexity so that you can maximise your financial benefits while minimising the risks.

Why worry? The government will look after me ...

Yes, the government will look after you if you make no provision for yourself. However, the non-contributory state pension in Ireland is the minimum you need for survival – it won't fund anything extra. The current non-contributory state pension pays a maximum of €219 a week (increased to €229 after age eighty). It's means-tested, and additional earnings may reduce the level of payment.

The Combat Poverty Agency calculates that 63,000 people, or over 13 percent of older people, are experiencing pensioner poverty. In a submission on the Green Paper on Pensions (June 2008), the agency states that the level of poverty among older people is closely linked to the level of the state pension. The agency is concerned that pensioner poverty may increase as the number of pensioners in the economy grows to an expected 1.24 million in 2036 from the current figure of under 0.5 million (2006). Financing these pensions will put significant extra pressure on the Exchequer and may force the government to reduce the value of pensions in real terms.

The current non-contributory state pension does not stretch to paying for holidays, meals out, or tickets for the cinema or shows. Those living on it have little to spare to buy presents for grandchildren or any other small luxuries. If the value of the pension is squeezed further then it will offer little quality of life for those dependent upon it.

If you want a decent standard of living in your retirement then you'll need to provide it for yourself – in part or fully. This guide explores how you'll achieve this.

I'll worry about my retirement tomorrow . . .

Some see planning for their retirement as something that they'll do sometime in the future; maybe shortly before the actual day that they retire. That's a big mistake for two reasons. Firstly, the later you leave it, the more it costs. Secondly, you rule out the possibility of retiring earlier or achieving some of the dreams that you harbour for your later years.

The sooner you start planning for your retirement, the easier it is to achieve your objectives. If you are saving for a particular purpose, then the longer that you save, the easier it becomes. If you are putting money into a pension scheme, then the sooner you start, the less it will cost and the greater the potential benefit will be. For example, you'll need to invest approximately 15 percent of your salary if you start a pension scheme at the age of twenty-five to fund a pension equal to 66 percent of your salary. You'd have to invest close to 40 percent if you start your pension fund at forty-five years of age.

Saving, too, is easier if spread over a long period. You can also benefit from better interest rates if you are able to leave your money untouched for longer periods.

Not all of us remain in the same employment throughout our lives. We may experience periods of unemployment or times when resources are so scarce that we cannot afford to add to our pensions or savings. Those who establish these saving and investment habits early have the option of taking a break from contributing when times are tough. Money invested in a pension fund or long-term savings product should continue to grow even if you are not adding to the initial capital.

The later you start planning, the fewer your options. At forty-five, you have only ten years until the age of fifty-five – making it very difficult to provide adequately for retirement at that age: you have little time to build up the necessary funds or put in place the systems that you need to achieve the retirement you want.

It's best therefore to start preparing for retirement earlier rather than later. This doesn't mean that you spend your whole working life thinking about what you'll do when you retire, but you should concentrate on building up funds in your earlier years and decide how you'll use them in your later ones.

There may be trouble ahead

The Celtic Tiger is well and truly dead and buried (in a vacant development site). Many are facing a new and frightening reality where their incomes decline, the value of their investments drops, property prices tumble and state help declines. It is tempting to give up on plans for our retirement, especially if it is far-off, and concentrate on the immediate problems that face us.

This is a foolish approach. Essentially, you would be giving away control over your future, and committing yourself to a life of dependency, either on others or on the possibility of a future boom providing for your needs. A well-known politician may have once described the Celtic Tiger boom as getting 'boomier', but there is nothing to stop the post-Celtic Tiger bust from getting 'bustier'.

The current recession is squeezing the government's finances and ensuring that we will continue to carry a large debt burden well into the future. There is plenty of evidence to suggest that present and future governments will do less and less to help people provide for their futures. Recent government-commissioned reports suggest that there will be less and less assistance given to those providing for their own future and that many of the benefits already in place will be reduced or phased-out altogether. And, of course, we have already seen the government remove pensioners' automatic right to a medical card. We can also assume that other benefits currently taken for granted – such as fuel allowances, carers' allowances etc – will be cut or made subject to a means test.

It seems inevitable that pensions for public sector employees will shift from the highly attractive defined benefit (where you are guaranteed a set percentage of your final salary) to the defined contribution (where your pension is based on the value of the contributions you have made over the life of the fund – without any guarantee of a minimum value) or some other less attractive option. There is also a likelihood that the tax relief for pension contributions will be reduced to the standard income tax, requiring that the individual either increase their contribution or lose some of the benefits that they could obtain. Another proposal is that lump-sum gratuities should be taxed, at least in part. These proposals (and their serious consideration) point to government being less inclined to support those investing and saving for their golden years. They also suggest that those who have planned on the basis of expecting some of these benefits may have to radically alter their thinking.

Planning is far more important when resources are scarce than when they are in abundance. We may have to adjust our plans or change the route we choose to achieve them. This may require exploring new or different alternatives to those we had settled upon. You may not be able to buy and live in a villa in southern Italy anymore, but you may still be able to enjoy a much less expensive Mediterranean idyll in Montenegro or Croatia. Those who have already started saving and investing have something to build upon and have some of the leverage needed to make a change.

A silver lining?

Remember that a recession may provide opportunities, too. For example, those in secure state employment may be offered incentives to leave early. These opportunities may allow you to begin fulfilling your dreams sooner. Those with a clear idea of what they want for their future will be better placed to take advantage of such opportunities and negotiate deals that suit their specific needs.

There may also be more opportunities for arrangements such as flexible working. This may suit those who wish to retire but want stay in the workforce in some way. It may also offer a route for those wishing to establish a part-time business of their own. The earnings from part-time work coupled with more free time may provide an opportunity for entrepreneurial activity.

And, of course, the cost of buying or renting property has also dropped. This makes purchasing easier and also allows people to find a house that more closely suits their needs.

2

Planning for Your Golden Years

'When I retire . . .'

How many times have you heard friends and colleagues beginning a sentence with this or a similar phrase? Unfortunately, that's as far as most of us get in planning for our later years. Yet, with some thought and careful planning, we may be able to turn those dreams into reality.

The quality of your retirement depends on how you prepare for it beforehand. Financial security comes from careful planning or extraordinary luck – such as winning the Lotto or being born into a wealthy family. There are three important questions that you must answer when planning for your later years:

- How much will I need to survive?

- What do I want to do and what will it cost?

- What have I done so far to prepare for my later years?

What you'll absolutely need

We need money to live. Our core expenses – food, drink and shelter – will still be there as we age, and some of them will increase with time. There is a myth that the basic cost of living declines with age. This is not necessarily the case: while we may eat less, energy and fuel costs will rise if we are spending a greater proportion of our time at home. Home maintenance costs increase as properties age and if they are used more. Health and medical expenses can increase, too.

The media regularly carry stories of older people struggling to survive on the means at their disposal. Your first objective in planning for your golden years should be to ensure that you have sufficient funds to pay for your basic needs and to give you some minimum comforts. The non-contributory state pension is barely enough to meet these needs; and those living on it may need additional help just to survive. The CSO annual survey of household incomes shows that older people living alone are at greater risk of poverty than most other groups: close to a quarter of this group are at risk of poverty. Coupled with the information from Combat Poverty given earlier, it's clear that most of us will need more than the basic non-contributory state pension.

So how much will you need to survive? The following table gives a short list of the main costs we must pay to survive:

	Expense	Approximate Cost
Food and drink	What you need for a healthy, balanced diet	
Clothing	Summer	
	Winter	
Energy and fuel costs	Electricity	
	Town gas	
	Heating oil, bottled gas	
	Petrol and/or public transport expenses	
Rent/mortgage costs	Mortgage or rent	
	Mortgage protection policy	
Property charges	Waste charges	
	Property taxes	
Home maintenance	Cleaning materials	
	Painting and decorating	
	Repairs (plumbing, electric, etc)	
Communications	Fixed line/mobile phone	
	Cable television	
	TV licence	
	Internet connection	
Healthcare	Health insurance	
	Home help where it is needed	
	Consultations/treatments not covered by insurance	
	Prescription costs up to threshold	
	Paramedical costs, etc (e.g. physiotherapy)	
	Total	

Now look at what you spend on each of these at present. Take food, for example: calculate how much you spend as a household on food per person, per week. Then, if you are a couple, multiply this by two. Include some compensation if one or both of you eat out regularly. Remember too that food costs more when bought in smaller portions: if you currently buy packages for a family of four, then the unit cost will increase if you are buying smaller amounts.

Calculate your energy and fuel costs based on spending all of your time at home, if you work away from home at present. If you work from home, use your current expenditure; if you work away from home, multiply your current costs by two. If you are now renting, then assume that this cost will continue. If you have a mortgage, then you know when you'll finish your repayments and you can make an allowance for this.

You may be surprised – or indeed scared – at the size of this figure when you add up all of the individual items. It will probably come to somewhere between €15,000 and €25,000 in present values (2009–2010) for a couple; and for some it may be considerably more.

Remember that this figure only includes the basic cost of living. It leaves out extras such as running a car, which may be an essential if there is no public transport in the area where you live. Holidays, family events, presents, and occasional treats or luxuries are excluded, too.

This figure is the absolute minimum you'll need to survive. To enjoy your golden years, what you really need to find out is what you *want*.

How much will you need to enjoy your golden years?

Working out what you need to survive is straightforward enough. Calculating what you want is more complicated. The real skill in planning for your golden years is to make sure that what you put aside is sufficient to fund what you want to do in the future, without preventing you from doing what you want to do in the present.

We all have dreams of what we'd like to do when we retire or reach our later years. But dreams will remain as such if we don't put plans in place to make them a reality. We must decide too what is realistic as opposed to fantasy; for example, you are unlikely to take up mountaineering and climb Mount Everest in your retirement if you have never gone mountain climbing before.

We can have other dreams that are possible, but which will need careful planning to achieve. For instance, you may wish to live abroad for all or part of your retirement. While achievable, you'll have to research such a move carefully and discuss it with others who will be affected by your decision. Major changes such as this have tax and other regulatory consequences that you will have to take into consideration.

You really need to think seriously about how you are likely to spend your time when you retire. And you should do this as early in your live as is practical. You may be an enthusiastic golfer, but do you really want to spend all of your time on the greens? And what of the costs? You'll have membership and green fees, travel costs, and of course all of the additional expenses – clubs, balls, bar, meals etc – that you'll incur as a regular golfer.

Envisioning the future

Try to imagine how you'd like to spend your later years and use this as the basis for projecting your financial needs. Do you dream of retiring to an apartment in Spain or a country cottage in the west of Ireland? Or perhaps you intend to sail around the world single-handed. Some may simply want to tackle their garden or build an extension on their home.

Do a bit of brainstorming. Take a sheet of paper and write down all of the things that you might like to do. Put everything down – there are no barriers. Use this sheet as a basis for talking to family and friends about what they think you may like. You should discuss this carefully with a partner, if you have one, and listen carefully to what they want to do, too.

The major projects require special planning (we will deal with these later); for now, we'll concentrate on the day-to-day expenses that we will experience.

Calculate the costs of hobbies and other activities. Think about how much you'll spend on social activities: evenings out, social drinks, tickets for shows, and presents for family and friends need to be budgeted for, too.

You will have other regular expenses. A car, if you have one, needs to be replaced at regular intervals. It costs money to run, maintain, insure and tax. Holidays are another potential expense that you should budget for.

Those retiring may wish to take up an entirely new

pursuit. You may want to learn a new skill, such as playing a musical instrument; or you may decide to pursue your education further. Tuition fees and other educational expenses mount-up quickly.

You should also allow some extra money for unexpected expenses that may crop-up. Those with family members may want to help a son or daughter buy a home or set up in business. Parents or older dependents may need your support at some later stage and you might like to make provisions for this.

You are now in a position to calculate what you will need to fund the retirement that you want.

Use the table on the next page to work out how much you would need today to fund the lifestyle you'd like in your retirement. Use today's values when doing this and avoid making allowances for inflation. Obviously, you don't know exactly what you want to do, so make provisions for a range of possibilities.

For most people, the total comes as a surprise – and sometimes an unpleasant one at that. We tend to underestimate our living expenses, especially in an environment where our income increases ahead of our costs.

Of course, you won't incur all of these expenses every year. You may only change your car every few years and you may not plan to go back to education. Use this to estimate what is the most you are likely to spend in any one year and then work out the possible average. You have to provide for the occasional more-expensive year at the time and you therefore need to have savings or the possibility of borrowing to do so.

These figures are guesstimates – they aren't exact calculations. They are based on the assumption that

	Expense	Approximate Cost
Basic needs	See calculation from page 22 above	
Car	Insurance	
	Motor tax	
	NCT Replacement annualised	
	Running costs (e.g. petrol and maintenance)	
Holidays	Travel	
	Accommodation	
	Spending money	
Leisure	Meals out, drinks, taxies	
	Show tickets	
	Books	
Recreational pursuits	Membership fees	
	Clothing and equipment	
Hobbies (e.g. gardening, collecting, etc)	Supplies and equipment	
Courses/training	Fees/tuition, books	
	Meals and other associated expenses	
Family commitments	Birthday and wedding presents	
	Help with children's home purchase	
Other expenses	One-off treats	
	Once in a lifetime events	
	Total	

certain costs will remain the same in real terms and that you won't incur any major additional expenses, such as the need to pay for home care in case of illness. They also exclude major changes in prices, such as the cost of fuel and other goods or services. Financial forecasting is never going to be wholly accurate, but these estimates allow you to develop your plans. We'll look at inflation-proofing and being prepared for the unexpected in later chapters.

How much will you have to live on?

You now need to address the final part of the jigsaw: namely, how much will you have to live on in your retirement, based on what you've put in place for the future already.

If you have a pension, how much will it be worth upon your retirement? You need to look at your pension scheme carefully and check what benefits it will deliver. Are they guaranteed and secure? Will you receive a lump-sum payment? Are you entitled to a contributory state pension? What other benefits are you entitled to? Your employer may also have made some additional provisions for you, such as health insurance, and you should list these.

Next, list your other savings and investments. Do you have one or more properties, and do they yield an income? What other investments, such as shares or other funds, do you have and what are their values now and likely values in the future? What restrictions are there on encashing these and how will you receive benefits from them? Do you have money in a bank or savings account – again, what are they earning at present and what will they yield in the future?

Have you any other sources of income or potential income and what is its value? For example, you may have land leased that yields an income or a share in a family farm that provides an income or will be of value at some later stage. You may also expect an inheritance or some other financial windfall. You may include these in your calculations, but be careful that you don't over-estimate their potential value or the likelihood of receiving them.

You may also have other valuables such as works of art or antiques. Although valuable, don't include them in your calculations unless you are certain you would be willing to sell them at some stage.

Calculate your potential income sources:

- Will you receive a state contributory pension? If so, what value will it have?

- What value will your personal pension have?

- What about a retirement lump sum?

- Do you anticipate having significant savings or inheritances?

- Do you have investments yielding an income?

- Have you other income streams that will continue into retirement?

- What about valuables that you would be willing to sell?

Now compare what you have put aside with what you want for your golden years.

Keep an eye on the risks that you face

You also need to include an evaluation of the potential risks and uncertainties associated with your income streams. While calculations of potential expenditure are usually reasonably certain, those for likely income can be a lot shakier. You need to consider:

- How secure is your pension?

- Is the value calculated for your retirement date realistic?

- How much of your pension fund is in riskier investments, such as shares and/or company bonds?

- Are your investment risks spread out over a number of sectors and regions? Is one share or fund dominant?

- How well is any property letting likely to perform in the future?

- Are there any special risks, such as flooding, that may reduce the value of investment properties?

- How secure is the bank in which you hold your savings?

- Is there a strong market for any valuables you may plan to sell?

There are likely to be further costs that you will face in the future and you need to factor these in too. Property taxes will expand – probably to all private property – and increase over the next decade. There may also be extra taxation and a reduction in the benefits that citizens can expect to get for the taxes that they pay. Average interest rates will rise over the next decade from the present, abnormally low ones. You need to factor in an additional 5 percent (approximately) as a cushion to cover these potential costs.

Once you've made your calculations, you can compare and contrast what you'll want with the funds that you'll have in place by the time you reach retirement. If the two figures match – well done. If not, you need to read on.

3

Working on Your Dream

Planning for your retirement takes time and deserves attention. It isn't necessarily something that you can do all at once and it is definitely best done well in advance of your retirement date.

People take contrasting approaches to retirement planning. The following two very different approaches summarise the range of attitudes people have to retirement planning. The first are those people who work flat-out until the day of their retirement. They have no plans for the future and crash into their retirement without any idea of what they want to do. They stop working one day with nothing planned for the following days, weeks or years. Lacking the structure of the world of work, the retiree is left trying to find things to do to fill their days. If someone retires having been the sole breadwinner with a partner at home, then they may find that their presence at home becomes a cause of conflict, as they get in the way of well-established routines. Unoccupied, the retiree may become prone to boredom, restlessness, irritability and physical or psychological illness, such as depression.

The second extreme are those people who build fantasies around their later years. They dream of all that they will do when the day comes. They may plan to travel the world; become an expert archaeologist; write a bestselling novel or even seek election as a politician. But unless they have done something to progress their dreams long before they retire, they will often remain just that: dreams. Even if they embark upon their dreams and schemes, their lack of preparation can turn those dreams into nightmares.

This is not to say that you shouldn't dream – far from it. What you have to do is take the next step and begin working to make your dreams reality. Some questions may help you to clarify your thinking about what you may want to do in your later years. Use this table to help you to work out what you want to do in your years of retirement.

Question	Answer
Do you plan to give up working when you retire?	
If you stay in employment, do you plan to stay in the same job or sector but work shorter hours?	
Do you want to take up different employment? Have you a clear idea of what that might be?	
What do you enjoy doing now and how much time will you spend on this in your retirement?	

(table continued)

33

Do you want to stay living in the same place or do you want to move somewhere else?	
Have you any dreams or wishes that are unfulfilled but which you are determined to fulfil?	
Who else is involved in your plans? What are their plans, and are the two compatible?	
What duties or responsibilities are you still likely to have and how will these affect your plans?	
What other calls (such as babysitting grandchildren) are there likely to be on your time?	

Continuing to work

Not everyone wants to give up work when they pass the age of sixty-five. A lot of people are fulfilled by the work that they do and cannot countenance giving up the world of work. However, they may not want to work all of the time or at the same job or with the same amount of pressure. There are also those who may have to continue working in some way because they don't have the financial wherewithal to retire.

We'll deal with detailed financial and personal planning for continuing to work in Chapter 5, but let's now look at the key points for those planning to continue working into their later years.

The first decision point you may face is whether you want to continue in the same job, organisation or sector as the one that you work in at present. Some organisations have an upper age limit and require people to retire when they reach it. This doesn't mean that you have to quit the area entirely, but it may require you to undergo a radical change in your role.

It's worth exploring your work opportunities in your own organisation well in advance of your retirement. Look at what others before you have done in your situation. Are there retirees working part-time or as consultants? Talk to them and find out how they have achieved this. Check too whether they are happy with their arrangements and what they might perceive as being the drawbacks to their current situation.

You should find out what your company's policies are about working in your later years. Discuss it with your human resource management to get a sense of their approach. Remember that there are great benefits for employers in retaining staff beyond retirement age: there are no recruitment costs; they know their older employees and what they can expect of them; older employees have built up a wealth of experience and an employer benefits from this through its direct use and the mentoring that older staff members provide to younger recruits.

Continuing in your employment

- Start planning early
- Check your company's policy on part-time working or returning to work as a consultant
- Are there any organisation policies that will prevent you from working after your retirement date?

- What impact will these policies have on your pension and other benefits?

- What has the experience been like for others who have been in similar situations?

Not everyone wants or will be able to continue in their current employment. If you plan to continue working, then you should start planning well before you reach your retirement date. You may want to stay in the same broad field, or you may want to take up something completely different. There is also the possibility that you may want to use the skills you have in a different way.

Continuing to work in the same area, but with different people, requires preparation and careful consideration. You must establish whether your employer can restrict you in any way. You may work in a company with high levels of intellectual property or industrial secrets and your employer may limit what you can do once you leave. This is rarely the case, but you should identify this early rather than discover it later, when you have started putting your plans into action.

You need to look at your qualifications and skill base if you plan to start afresh. Even though you may have attained a very high skill level in your profession, you may still find it difficult to demonstrate these to others. You should consider taking up evening or part-time courses to upgrade your skills or acquire necessary new ones. Look too at the work that you've done and identify areas where you you've gained important skills that may be of use to a potential employer. For example, you may have taken part in the introduction of a quality system such as

ISO 9000 and so have competencies that another organisation may value. You may wish to train further in your chosen field and you should examine how you will achieve that.

Some of us may have started our working lives with certain technical or specialist skills but subsequently moved on to supervisory or management positions. Check your qualifications and establish how up-to-date these are. Continuing professional development will hone your skills and make you a more attractive employment prospect.

Training and development is time-consuming and may be challenging for those who haven't been involved in it for a long time. You should take it in easy-to-manage stages and build up your capability gradually. Attaining a qualification through evening or part-time courses takes two- to three-times as long as a full-time course; you may find it takes more out of you than you expect. Allow plenty of time to develop the skills you need or want: you may take several years to build up your skills to the level you seek and you should make sure that you factor long-term training into your retirement plan.

Skills in themselves are not all you need. You should also build up or reinvigorate your professional network. Apply for membership to technical or professional bodies if you aren't already a member of any. Attend these bodies' meetings or social events as well as other good networking opportunities, such as trade fairs and exhibitions relating to your work.

You may wish to raise your professional profile. There are simple steps that that you may take that can help you to do this, such as becoming actively involved in trade organisations, institutes, trade unions or other bodies that will bring your name to the attention of your peers. Business organisations like your local chamber of commerce offer ideal opportunities to meet other business people in your area who may be seeking your skills. Volunteering for positions of responsibility in local chambers or trade, technical and professional bodies also raises your profile. Think too about promoting yourself through articles in trade and technical presses. You may also wish to consider taking a part-time position teaching – for example working in the evening in an institute or college. Educational institutes often look for experienced people to deliver training on practical courses.

You may also wish to branch out on your own after retiring. We'll examine that option later when we look at setting up your own business. However, much of the same advice applies as regards skills, contacts, profile etc. And it's likely that you'll need a very much broader network when you are looking for business on your own.

Preparing to work in another organisation

- Check that there aren't any contractual restrictions on working for another employer after your retirement

- Strengthen your skills base

- Update your professional qualifications

- Strengthen your network among peers in your sector

- Volunteer for positions in trade and professional bodies to build up your profile and demonstrate your abilities

- Write articles and pieces for trade and technical publications and websites

- Check to see if there are teaching opportunities in local colleges and institutes.

And now for something completely different

Our golden years present us with an opportunity to make a break from our comfort zones and try something completely different. In some cases it may be a means to an end; in others it may be the end in itself. A former colleague of mine wanted to travel in his retirement. He was keen to get to know in depth the places he visited and to spend time in them, getting to understand the life and culture. He determined to pay his way by teaching English as a foreign language. He prepared for this well in advance and studied for an internationally recognised qualification in Teaching English as a Foreign Language (TEFL). He built up his experience by teaching part-time in the evenings in the years prior to his retirement so that, when he actually retired, he was well qualified and had the confidence to take on a completely different career.

Others may wish to turn their hobby or interest into a way of earning extra cash and keeping themselves active and involved in their retirement. If you are an enthusiastic gardener, then you could improve your skills, receive some professional training and offer a gardening service in your locality. The same holds true for those who are good at DIY: there are probably households in your area looking for someone to carry out minor repairs or improvements. Look at what you're good at and what you enjoy doing and then see if there is a market somewhere for these talents.

It's best to think about establishing yourself before you retire. Again, consider evening or weekend work in your final years in your current employment. Get to know others in the same line of work and find out if they want someone as a part-time or temporary worker. Such experience gives you a very clear idea of whether you would really like to spend your later years working in that way and also whether you are really suited to your new career.

Dreams do come true

Many of us have dreams of things we wish to do or achieve in our golden years. As mentioned, these will stay dreams if we don't prepare and plan in order to succeed. If we want to occupy our later years pursuing a hobby or interest, and we are not earning any income from it, then the chances are that it will cost us.

Avoid telling yourself that you'll take up a new hobby or pastime when you retire. For instance, you may believe that you would love to be an artist on your retirement. If this is something that you really want to do, then start preparing immediately. Don't waste twenty years dreaming only for it to be shattered in your first week of retirement when you discover you can't draw. Attend evening classes. Start painting or sculpting in the evenings and at weekends. Pay attention to the practical details: find out how much it costs, what time it takes to produce the work of the quality that you aspire to and whether you really enjoy doing it. You may even consider producing work for sale or public viewing and this could help make the hobby self-funding.

In any case, don't invest too much in something that you are unsure of, even before you retire. Buy or borrow second-hand equipment, attend introductory courses rather than signing up for a year-long (or longer) commitment, etc. Dip your toe in the water before you take the plunge.

The big project

There are some people who have a major ambition for their retirement – a major project that will absorb all of their time and effort and will fulfil a long-held dream. It may be that you want to build your own home in your idyllic place; start farming and become self-sufficient; maybe you dream of sailing around the world.

You *can* achieve these dreams, as long as you start working on them long before your retirement begins. You will do them in your later years – but you'll lay the foundations for them now. The most important thing to do is to create a project plan with set milestones that you want to achieve. You should start planning in the decade prior to your retirement and embarking on your great adventure.

You'll realise your dreams in the same way you'll achieve anything else in life. Start by researching what's involved. You can begin this years before you intend to start out. Carry out some trials – test yourself to see whether you can actually do what it is you want to do. If you want to sail around the world, then maybe you test yourself sailing around Ireland, or crossing to France or Spain. Get training in the skills that you'll need and make sure that you have the opportunity to practice them.

Begin investing as early as possible. Buy the site if you want to build a house and start the planning permission process. The yachter may want to buy and equip an appropriate craft. It's better to spread out costs over a prolonged period and try to take advantage of any offers or market downturns over the years. All the time keep your focus on your overall goal.

Major projects will need support from family and friends. You will also need colleagues, friends or workers with specific skills and their willingness to give these to you. A person planning to build their own perfect home will benefit greatly from the help of skilled craftspeople. And so you should look at ways in which you could involve them in the project over the years leading up to your retirement.

We'll look at how to finance your dreams, be they major or minor, over the next chapters and see how we can blend the funding with the enjoyment of the funds.

Planning to turn dreams into reality

- Define clearly what it is you want to achieve

- Find out whether you really want to spend your time doing the work that it requires

- Start training and carrying-out trial runs and experiments

- Start investing early in the essentials that you will need

- Build the network you'll need to support you when you come to put your plan into action

- Get started if you can – and long before your retirement date.

Planning together

You may be one half of a couple. And you may intend to stay in your relationship into your retirement and old age. If so, then you'd better make sure that your plans are shared and meet both of your needs fairly.

Couples generally have a way of living and working together. If one of you works in the home or in a home office, then that is his or her workplace, and problems may arise when the other retires and starts being in the home all of the time. You need to prepare for this eventuality. If not, one or both of you may find the new situation difficult to cope with.

You should discuss each of your wants and needs well in advance of the time for retirement. Take account of each other's personal space and time. Consider how you will manage your finances jointly and fairly. If both of you have worked and have pension rights, what are they? And are they equal?

Couples should be clear about each other's retirement plans. In particular, you should both agree on common finance arrangements. If you've lived separately, each managing your own money, then you may need to examine the prospect of pooling your finances and re-examining your needs. If you have two cars, then may you wish to consider whether you'll need both after one or both retires. And if you are planning to get rid of a car, then you should make this decision well in advance so that you plan your later purchases together and appropriately.

Given the reduction in overall household income after retirement, couples should make sure that they have a clear and common understanding of what each wants, both financially and in how each plans to spend his or her time.

Other responsibilities may have implications

We need to consider our other responsibilities when planning our finances for retirement. We may have to care for parents, partners or children who become or continue to be dependent for the foreseeable future. While there are state supports available, these are seldom sufficient to provide for those with severe disabilities or ongoing illnesses like dementia; we have to factor in provisions for our dependents' continuing needs – for some, even after death.

We may also wish to help our children build their own lives and create a solid financial foundation for their future. For example, you might plan to help them through post-graduate education, finance a business start-up or give them the deposit for a home. Post-graduate fees are often over €5,000 a year. while a deposit for a home will be tens of thousands of euro.

Those with a business may wish to pass it on to their children, and there will be financial conse- quences to this. Careful financial planning will help you maximise the amount you can pass on to the next generation.

Couples may also want to have the reassurance that the remaining partner will have a secure life following one or the other's death. This involves more than just inheritance planning, as there are steps that you can take to prepare for this eventuality. We'll return to this topic at a later stage.

The remainder of this book looks at how you can manage your finances for your golden years. It will explore what you can do to build up your wealth; how you can use it to the maximum benefit and how you can make allowances for unforeseen circumstances.

4

Getting the Money You Need to Provide the Lifestyle You Want

There are four core sources of the wealth that you'll need to fund your retirement:

- Pension
- Investment
- Savings
- Assets (such as property or business)

Of course, a pension is usually nothing more than a combination of savings and investments (although technically state pensions are taken out of current government funds). We treat them different because pension provision receives different tax treatment.

Each of the above is important in your overall preparation for your golden years. You need to examine how dependent you are on each component and understand what risks are associated with them. Sadly, for example, the 2008 financial crash exposed the weakness of depending on shares in only one company as a source of retirement income. We heard distressing stories of people in their later years left almost destitute when the dividend cheques from their banks stopped coming.

We'll look carefully at the risks associated with each source of income in providing for our later years. The point I want to stress throughout is the need to ensure there is a balance between our different funding methods and the levels of risk we are exposed to by them.

A good, pensionable job . . .

For many of my generation, the baby-boomers, the common piece of career advice we received from our parents was to find and keep a good, pensionable job. It is only now, in post-crash Ireland, that we really understand what our parents were concerned about, and what motivated them in proffering that advice: they had lived through a turbulent time and experienced directly or indirectly the impact of prolonged economic recession, even depression. Perhaps they had even seen or heard of wealthy people rendered destitute by the Wall Street crash of the late 1920s. Given their experience of uncertainty, it's not surprising that they emphasised financial security so strongly.

A pension is an excellent way of providing for your later years. It is tax-efficient, has certain legal protection, can be an automatic benefit of employment and in certain cases it is provided by the state.

What is a pension?

That's not as simple to answer as you'd think. There are two sources of pensions: private pension schemes and state-provided ones. Within these, there are further subdivisions. Private schemes may be based on giving a definite benefit on retirement or on what you have invested in a fund over a period of time. State-funded pensions are either granted as a benefit, on foot of paying Pay Related Social Insurance (PRSI), or assistance, based on a means-tested assessment of need. Basically, a pension is a stream of income that will provide for your later years. It can have two components: a lump sum and a regular payment. The value of and the length of time a pension is paid may depend upon the value of the pension pot created.

What the State provides

As mentioned, the State provides two main forms of retirement pension: the contributory and the non-contributory state pensions. The contributory pension is an entitlement established through the payment of Pay Related Social Security (PRSI). The non-contributory pension is given as assistance or an allowance, and you do not contribute directly towards it. In addition, there are other specific pension schemes for the blind, the disabled, the widowed, and homemakers. We will not deal with these in this book, but people who believe that they fall into these categories should contact the Department of Social and Family Affairs to find out whether they are eligible.

State pension schemes are complex and we will only address the main points here. Also, remember that we are using the current schemes as our source of information. These may change significantly by the time you reach the age to start benefitting from them. The government generally sets the value of the state pensions at budget time, and this has increased gradually in recent years. However, the change in Ireland's finances may result in the value being let to decline in real terms. Be careful about basing your pension planning solely around the state pension schemes.

Contributory state pension

The contributory state pension (officially known as the State Pension (Contributory)) has the following key elements:

- it is not means tested
- you can have other sources of income while collecting it
- it is based on the social welfare contributions you've made
- payments begin after the age of sixty-six

The contributory state pension is an entitlement that you establish through paying your PRSI contributions (Classes A, E, F, G, H, N or S social insurance contributions). To qualify, you must:

- have commenced paying social insurance contributions before a certain date
- have paid a certain number of contributions
- reach a certain average number of payments per year since you began contributing

49

People under the age of sixty-six must have begun paying contributions before the age of fifty-six. Normally, the starting date is taken to be the date of your first paid contribution. There are complex rules applying to different, specific situations. Generally, where there is an element of uncertainty, the more favourable date is taken.

PRSI contributions: What you pay

Most employees over the age of sixteen pay social insurance contributions into the national Social Insurance Fund. Generally, these contributions are compulsory and the amount that you contribute depends upon the type of work that you do. If you are an employee, then your employer is responsible for collecting PRSI contributions from you. You pay part of it as an employee share while your employer pays the remainder of the contribution. Self-employed people pay their contributions directly to Revenue.

The rate of PRSI contribution you pay varies depending upon your earnings and your type of work. Those working in the state sector pay less than those in the private sector, while the self-employed have a different rate again. At the time of writing, the PRSI rate including a health levy for the first €52,000 is 6 percent for the private sector, 3.15 percent for the state sector, and 5 percent for self-employed. The next €48,100 is levied at 2 percent for the public and private sectors and 5 percent for the self-employed. Any remaining income is levied at 2.5 percent for the public and private sectors and 5 percent for the self-employed.

The amount that you pay varies, as do the benefits

that you derive from these payments. You should try to maintain your social insurance payments even when you aren't working as best you can. You are able to keep your social insurance record active, should you leave the workforce, through credited contributions whereby you are given a credit because you are not in employment. Again, you should check this with your local Social and Family Affairs office. You can even make voluntary contributions in certain circumstances where you are no longer paying compulsory contributions; there are specific rules covering both your entitlement to make contributions and the benefits that you may claim. Those who retire early should make sure that they either continue making their contributions or get credited contributions in order to maintain their pension entitlement. If you find yourself in any such situation, check with your local office or your accountant.

Self-employed

There are special rules for entry into social insurance for self-employed people. If you began your contributions on or prior to 6 April 1988 and had paid-employee insurance any time, then the date of entry into insurance is taken as either the 6 April 1988 or the date on which you first paid insurance – whichever is the most advantageous.

The number of PRSI contributions you need to have made

Part of your retirement planning may involve maximising your entitlement to a state contributory pension.

There are rules governing the number of contributions you need to have made prior to your retirement to entitle you to a pension, whether it is a full or a part-pension. These are complicated and depend upon your current age, your retirement age, your employment history and when you started paying contributions. This guide will give you an overview of the main rules, but you should check with your employer, your accountant or the Department of Social and Family Affairs to establish your exact entitlements.

To qualify for a contributory state pension you must have made a certain minimum number of contributions over a certain number of years. The exact number and the way in which these are determined depends upon when you started making the payments and your expected retirement date. Making these minimum contributions entitles you to a pension, but not necessarily a full pension.

Social Welfare operates a system called the 'normal average rule' to calculate your pension entitlement. This states that you must have an annual average of ten appropriate, weekly contributions (that is, ten contributions average in each year) from the year you first entered insurance (or from 1953 – whichever is later). A ten-contribution average entitles you to the minimum pension; you need a forty-eight average to get the maximum.

As already stated, you can get credits for periods when you are unemployed or ill. However, you need a minimum number of credits gained through working to qualify for the contributory state pension. People reaching pension age before 6 April 2012 must have two hundred and sixty paid contributions (equivalent to five years' contribution, but not necessarily consecutive ones). However, if you were a voluntary contributor on or before 6 April 1997, you only need 156 contributions if you have a yearly average of 20 contributions or above.

The regulations change for those retiring after 6 April 2012: you will have to have five hundred and twenty paid contributions (equivalent to ten years' paid contributions). Only half of these contributions may be voluntary ones. However, if you were a voluntary contributor before 6 April 1997 and with an annual average of ten contributions, you may meet the requirement if you have a total of 520 contributions, but only 156 of these need to be compulsory paid contributions.

You qualify for a full pension if you have an average of forty-eight or more contributions per year. You'll get 98 percent of the pension if your average is between twenty and forty-seven contributions. This drops to 75 percent for an average number of contributions between fourteen and nineteen. Average contributions between ten and fourteen will entitle you to half the full pension.

People who have worked in an EU country or in a country with a bilateral agreement with Ireland, under certain circumstances, may qualify for a pension as long as they meet certain criteria and the Department of Social and Family Affairs will provide information on this.

There is a special scheme for people who take time off work to care for family members, such as children under twelve or a person who is incapacitated. This is the Homemaker's Scheme, and it allows you to disregard up to twenty years in the calculation of your average annual contributions if you satisfy the criteria set down in the scheme. You need to apply at the end of a homecare year to benefit from this scheme. However, you should get full, up-to-date information from the Social Welfare and find out whether you will qualify when you are planning to take time-off to care for someone.

The transition state pension

People retiring at sixty-five and who have sufficient contributions are entitled to claim the transition state pension. You will transfer to the contributory state pension when you reach the age of sixty-six. You aren't allowed to work while you are receiving the transition pension, but you can work when you move to the contributory pension.

The non-contributory state pension

You qualify for this if:

- you are over sixty-six years of age
- you don't qualify for a contributory pension
- you pass a means test
- and you meet the habitual residence condition – that is, you are a permanent resident of Ireland.

The means test assesses your income from earnings, investments, and property. Your means are then added together to set your pension level. Couples' means are halved to establish the means of one of the couple. At present, the first €30 is not taken into account; but after that it is decreased by

€2.50 per week for every €2.50 of means.

There are some exceptions to the income assessed, such as payments under the Farm Retirement Scheme or income from property already assessed on its capital value. The non-contributory pension is restricted and intended only for those who have little or no other income and risk becoming destitute without it. You won't be able to plan a fulfilling retirement if you are depending upon it.

Getting to grips with your pension

The state pensions give a small and, for most people, inadequate income for what they might want to do in their later years. Most people aim to supplement the state benefits with some form of occupational pension. There is a wide variety of pension schemes available, though your choice will be affected by the scheme on offer where you work. Schemes vary hugely, so it's important that you find out exactly what the scheme you're in already, or are considering joining, offers its members.

Pension schemes can offer you significant financial benefits. You can avail of tax relief and in company schemes your employer may pay a significant part of your pension contribution – in other words, it's like an extra payment.

Tax treatment makes pension schemes attractive

Pension schemes are simply elaborate savings and/or investment schemes. It's their special treatment for tax purposes which makes them especially attractive. For example, companies can invest a certain amount into an employee's pension fund without the employee having to pay tax on it. The employee can invest a percentage of his or her earnings and gain tax relief on the amount. And you may be entitled to a tax-free lump sum (up to a certain amount) upon retirement. The major constraint that the government puts on pension funds is that, with certain exceptions, you must leave the money in the fund until you retire.

The government provides pensions tax incentives to encourage people to save for their later years so that the government won't have to provide for them from the public coffers. However, you should remember that these tax incentives are subject to change – you can't rely on cash-strapped administrations continuing to provide them into the future. For example, there is speculation that the value of lump sums may be capped and may be taxed. Others propose that the pension contributions should only receive tax relief at the lower tax rate. There is no guarantee that the government won't further reduce or eliminate special tax treatment for those saving for a pension, so it is better to take advantage of benefits that are there now, before it's too late.

The basics of pension schemes for employees

PAYE workers may be in a company pension scheme and this can deliver valuable benefits. One great advantage of a company-operated pension scheme is that any payments are deducted directly from your pay so that you aren't tempted to spend it.

There are two core types of company pension schemes: those with defined benefits and those with defined contributions. A defined benefit pension gives a set benefit on retirement. This is usually a set percentage of your final salary together with the payment of a lump sum on reaching your retirement age. Large organisations are usually the ones to offer defined benefit pensions. Most state employees have this type of pension. Banks and financial companies also offer or have offered these. The value of a defined benefit scheme lies in the fact that it protects the recipient from the vagaries of the financial markets and provides financial certainty on their retirement. Employers are attempting to move away from these schemes where possible and towards the riskier defined contribution scheme as these reduce the costs employers pay and also means that they don't have to provide for any shortfall in a pension fund.

In a defined contribution scheme, you contribute a set amount and this goes into a fund. The value of the fund determines what your pension will be worth at your retirement. Typically, you use the fund you've built up to purchase a pension from a financial institution. The main advantage of a defined contribution scheme is that it is portable. In other words, you take the real value of the scheme with you should you change employment. Defined contribution schemes give the employee the opportunity to benefit from market growth – the downside is obviously that he or she is exposed to market decline as well.

Upon taking up a job in a company, you should find out whether it has a pension scheme and whether you are eligible to join it. Eligibility varies from scheme to scheme, so you should establish this at the very outset or preferably even before you accept a position. In addition, you should get a clear statement of what the scheme includes. For example, many offer death-in-service benefits whereby your next of kin will receive a payment should you die while working for the company.

In most company schemes, the company pays part, if not all, of the contribution and the employee pays any remainder. The company contribution is tax free for the employee; the employee's contribution is usually tax free up to a certain percentage of his or her salary. Employers often pay the full contribution of a defined benefit scheme.

The current maximum contribution rates for employees (as a percentage of total salary) for which you may receive tax relief are as follows in these schemes:

Age during the tax year based on your upper age in the year	Rate for which you may receive tax relief
Under 30	15 percent
30–39	20 percent
40–49	25 percent
50–54	30 percent
55–59	35 percent
60 and over	40 percent

Should I join a company pension scheme?

The answer to this is nearly always yes – the main reason being that the company contributes to the fund and you benefit from a tax-free extra payment. You also benefit from the favourable tax treatment of your own contributions.

You are very unlikely to have a choice about the scheme offered by an employer. There is a trend for employers to change from defined benefit to defined contribution schemes. This is because companies are liable for the shortfall in a defined benefit scheme. This can prove expensive for them, and keeping funds solvent can prove problematical for some. You may also find that there are two types of schemes in operation in a company but only one of these will be open to new entrants.

Pension schemes may offer other benefits

You may find that your pension scheme offers other significant benefits. You may be entitled to up to two-thirds of your final salary. Your pension may continue to grow after you retire. It may be index-linked, meaning that it will increase in line with a financial index such as the rate of inflation. Often your pension increases by either a fixed percentage or an index – usually whichever is the lower. Pensions with a 'whichever is the lower' clause will actually decrease in value in real terms during periods of high inflation. For those who live to a ripe old age, this drop in value could be significant.

As mentioned, schemes usually have death-in-service coverage. Your next of kin may be entitled to a lump sum calculated as a multiple of your salary. They may receive a refund on your contributions, a spouse's or partner's pension, or in some cases a child's or orphan's pension. These are significant benefits, as they reduce the amount of money you would otherwise have to put aside to cover such eventualities, freeing up money for other forms of savings.

Those in defined contribution schemes should monitor their scheme closely to find out what benefit is can reasonably expect. You should receive an annual report on the scheme and this will set out what you can expect to achieve based on your fund's performance.

The money your company and you yourself put into a pension is generally managed by a fund management company, which aims to increase its value through shrewd investment. You should pay attention to how well the investment team performs. You may have to supplement the scheme, meaning that you will have to add money if the market underperforms. You may have to switch funds if the fund managers underperform and you feel that it is not achieving its objectives or doing as well as other funds.

What if you don't have access to an occupational pension scheme?

You may work in a company where there isn't a pension scheme at all. It's worth discussing this with your boss and exploring the possibility of setting one up, even if you end paying up to 90 percent of the contributions. Your employer can benefit from tax relief and does not have to pay PRSI payments on the contributions. Financial advisors from the major financial institutions will advise you on setting up a pension scheme and you can find independent advice on the Pensions Board website at *www.pensionsboard.ie.*

PRSAs

If all else fails, or if you are self employed, then you may set up your own personal pension plan. The Personal Retirement Savings Account (PRSA) is a mechanism that allows those without access to another form of pension scheme to provide for their old age. It also allows people to set up a pension for income that isn't covered by their current pension scheme.

You set up a PRSA with an authorised provider. Any adult can take out a PRSA and that includes employees, the self-employed, homemakers, carers and even those who are unemployed. This is a useful option for those who are outside the traditional world of work or are perhaps dipping in and out as freelancers or free agents. It is also one well worth looking at if you are self-employed.

An employer may contribute to a PRSA on behalf of an employee, but it's more usual for the individual to pay for the scheme themselves. As with other pension schemes, you benefit from tax relief on your contribution up to a maximum percentage of your income. These vary with age and are the same as those given to employees in a defined benefit scheme (shown in the table on page 58 earlier). There is a cap on earnings at €150,000, meaning that you cannot benefit from additional tax relief for earnings above this figure. However, at the other end of the scale you can claim €1,525 worth of tax relief regardless of income in the year. This is particularly useful for self-employed people who may experience significant shifts in their earnings caused by the irregular timing of payments.

One great advantage of PRSAs is that you can vary your contribution from one year to another depending upon your personal circumstances. You can either make regular contributions or pay one lump sum each year. Lump-sum investment suits the self-employed, whose incomes may vary.

You pay charges to the provider of a PRSA and these can be 5 percent of the contribution plus 1 percent of the assets under management for what is called a 'standard' PRSA. The fees are governed by pensions legislation. In these, your money must be invested in pooled funds, including unit trusts and life company unit funds two specific types of investment vehicles.

You may also invest in a 'non-standard' PRSA. These generally offer broader investment options – but possibly at a price, as there is no cap on the provider's charges. Most people will find that the standard PRSA suits their needs, but if you do opt for the non-standard make sure that you know what you will be charged both for on your contribution and for the management of the assets as these can be higher than those charged in the standard PRSA.

You may collect your benefits from your PRSA when you are between the ages of sixty and seventy-five. You may take these sooner in the event of retirement from employment after the age of fifty, or at any time should you become seriously ill (such that you will be unable to work in the future). You stop making contributions at the age of seventy-five.

Other schemes for particular needs

High earners may opt for setting up and managing the administration of their own funds. This is only practical for people with very large amounts of money available to them to put into a pension fund, as you also have to fund the scheme's administration from this. You also have to be certain that you are competent to manage the investments and/or that you trust your financial adviser fully. While these schemes can make a broad range of investments, there are certain assets that are excluded.

Pension mortgages were another popular pension option in the late nineties and early noughties. These are best suited to the self-employed or company directors. The individual takes out an interest-only mortgage on a property (usually a property for rental) and uses his or her pension lump sum to pay off the mortgage on retirement. You pay both the interest on the capital and contribute to a pension plan and the rental income from the property is offset against the interest repayments. These schemes are very tax-efficient, but obviously depend upon the strength of the property market both in terms of rental income and also potential growth in the value of a property. In addition, you are also gambling that the pension fund will grow sufficiently to pay off the initial capital sum borrowed.

People who own their own company can set up a director's pension plan. These are much more tax-efficient and the company can usually contribute a lot more than you could under a personal pension plan. These schemes are more flexible, both in terms of contribution and in how you take your benefits.

Building up your pension fund

As stressed, you should monitor your pension fund carefully to make sure that it will provide sufficient funds for the retirement that you want. If you find that the fund is insufficient or that you won't have worked a sufficient number of years to entitle you to a full pension, then you have the opportunity to build up your funds in another way.

You can make additional voluntary contributions, commonly called 'AVCs', to an occupational pension scheme where you want to maximise your retirement fund. You are entitled to tax relief on these, subject to the limits given in the tables earlier. These are a very efficient way of saving for your pension, especially where you receive tax relief at the higher level, because when you take the tax relief and PRSI into account you get approximately half of your investment back. It's best to make an AVC earlier rather than later, as the money will have longer to grow and you also benefit from the tax reliefs in place – but remember that these may change. You can, though, make AVCs right up to your retirement and claim tax relief over two years – you can claim back tax from past year as well as the current year. There are specific regulations governing AVCs and you should check with your financial advisor or those responsible for your pension within your company to find out how they apply in your case.

Public service pensions

The civil service pension is probably one of the best perks available to civil and many public servants, such as members of An Garda Síochána. The pension is the defined benefit type and may pay a tax-free lump sum of 1.5 times the final salary as well as a pension valued at 50 percent of the final salary. This is linked to the civil service pay scale so that it increases in line with general increases in pubic service pay. Thus, it is possible for retired civil servants to have a pension that exceeds their final salary after a relatively short period. In addition, civil servants can contribute to a spouse's pension worth a quarter of the finishing salary should the retiree die.

Those working in the civil or public service should make sure that they understand the scheme and the benefits they will receive. Consider 'buying back' years through additional contributions, AVCs, if you won't have worked a sufficient number of years to qualify for a full pension. You should also check what impact programmes, such as career-breaks or term-time working, will have on your pension entitlements.

Managing your pension investment

Large pension schemes have trustees and/or investment managers in place to manage or look after their funds. The trustees usually delegate the management of pension funds to investment managers, who take care of its day-to-day administration. The trustees are still responsible for the scheme and the management of the fund. The trustees should produce an annual report setting out how the scheme is performing. They will also make sure that payments are made and that individuals are aware of their personal standing. A well-managed scheme will ensure that there is an appropriate balance between risk and return.

Companies guarantee the benefits in defined benefit schemes. However this is not the case in defined contribution ones: so those in such schemes need to monitor the value of their fund regularly and decide what to do if it looks likely that it won't meet their needs.

What is a fund?

Those with personal pensions need to pay close attention to how their money is invested and the levels of risk that they are exposed to. Your pension money is generally invested in a fund established by a financial institution. A 'fund' is where a financial institution takes the individual contributions of fund members (you), combines them and invests the money in a range of assets. These assets are typically government bonds, stocks and shares, properties and other money instruments.

Usually, your financial advisor will offer you a choice of funds to invest your personal pension in. You will then generally select a spread of funds and decide what percentage of your contribution will go into each one. Remember: this is a personal choice and should reflect your age, market conditions and your own feelings about risk.

Funds on offer are usually categorised as:

- **Guaranteed** – with the capital protected and/or with a certain amount of growth guaranteed

- **Managed funds** – where investment managers move your money between assets in an attempt to maximise gains

- **Indexed funds** – that give you the same percentage growth or decline as occurs in a selected market (usually a stock market)

- **Property** – where your money is invested in a property portfolio which should yield rental income as well as a potential grow in value

- **Equities** – where the fund is invested in stock and shares directly in the market and you gain the benefits and suffer the losses resulting from the changes in value of these shares.

There are other funds, often referred to as 'specialist funds', which concentrate on very specific assets, such as precious metals.

Risk and return

There is a close relationship between the risk that your investment is exposed to and the return that you can hope to achieve from it. Generally speaking, the higher the risk, the greater the potential gain or loss. You may consider taking a greater risk when you have a long time to go until your retirement. This usually means investing in funds with a high proportion invested in equities. Equities generally show greater growth over the long term than other forms of investment. Certain funds smooth-out gains or losses in equities to give a more consistent return over the fund's life.

You should consider shifting to less-risky funds as you approach your retirement age, with the aim of consolidating your gains. These are usually guaranteed and invested in government-issued bonds. You should check the extent of the guarantee, as in some cases the guarantee may only be for a set period of time.

Discuss your plans with your adviser and establish the level of risk/reward that you are willing to accept. Avoid being swayed by current fashions or pressure to buy into the current star performer. Stars often burn brightest before they explode: and so it can be with funds – they often appear most attractive before they come crashing down to earth.

You pay for everything

You pay when you set up your pension fund and you'll pay for the fund's management. Remember that switching funds costs money and financial advisers generally receive a payment when they switch investments on behalf of a client. Make sure that the switch is to your advantage and contributes to real benefit to your fund.

Taking your money on retirement

Your retirement planning should take account of when and how you will receive your pension benefits. This is something that you should keep in mind when setting up your pension scheme.

Pension schemes may allow you to take a lump sum on retirement. With a personal pension plan you can take up to 25 percent of the fund tax free. Those in occupational schemes and with more than twenty years' service can receive a tax-free lump sum equivalent to a year and a half times their final salary. This amount reduces with fewer years' service.

Obviously, the more you take in a lump sum the less that you have as a pension. Those who have made AVCs to an occupational scheme can use them to supplement their lump sum (up to the one and half years of the final salary limit) or to add to their pension. Revenue allows you to count additional earnings, such as overtime and other earnings, when calculating your pension entitlements.

Those with personal pension plans, director's pensions, PRSAs or AVCs have to decide how to manage their remaining fund after the lump sum has been taken out. There are two core options: buy an annuity to provide a pension or invest it in a retirement fund.

An annuity is a policy that makes a series of payments to you until a specific event occurs. People use it to provide themselves with a guaranteed pension for the rest of their lives. It ends on the death of the holder but it can be structured so that it pays out on more than one life. Some annuities may guarantee to pay for a set number of years – often five years – and then cease once the person dies. It is paid to the next of kin for the remaining years if the holder should die within the five years.

Annuities are life assurance policies and are sold by licensed life assurance companies. You pay them money in return for an income stream. The companies calculate how long you are likely to live and work out what they can/will pay you based upon this calculation. They work on averages, so there is the possibility that you could make over your fund to a company by buying an annuity and, because of early death, and you or your next of kin receive relatively little of it. On the other hand, let's hope that you live well beyond your life expectancy and gain a great deal more than you invested. Some companies also offer 'impaired life annuity' products to people with medical conditions likely to shorten their life expectancy.

Normally, you can choose the features that form your annuity. You'll be able to set the length of a guarantee, whether you receive a fixed figure or whether it grows over time, etc. Each extra option costs money and thus reduces the value of your actual pension.

Instead of choosing an annuity, you may opt to put your money into a retirement fund. There are two options with these funds: an Approved Minimum Retirement Fund (AMRF) or an Approved Retirement Fund (ARF). These funds remain the pensioner's property (whereas as the life company takes your money and it then pays you a pension) although Revenue does have regulations governing their use. The main restriction in investment in a retirement fund is that, once you take your 25 percent lump sum, and the balance is less than €63,500, then you must put it into an AMRF if you don't put it into an annuity. Or you can split it between an AMRF and an annuity. For example, you may put €33,500 into an annuity and the remaining €30,000 into an AMRF.

There are two exceptions to the AMRF requirement. People over seventy-five don't have to invest in an AMRF. The second exemption is for people with an annual specified income greater than €12,700. A specified income has to be in place at retirement. Therefore, someone retiring at sixty years old can't use an anticipated social welfare pension expected at the age of sixty-five as a pension. The full AMRF investment requirement remains even if you have a pension less than the €12,700 threshold. You must invest the full €63,500 and cannot reduce it even if you have some form of pension.

You can't withdraw any of the initial capital that you invest in the AMRF, but you may take any gains that the fund earns. You'll pay income tax on anything that you take out of the scheme.

The regulations change for people once they reach the age of seventy-five (or on the death of the pensioner). At this point as long as you have met the requirements described already then you can receive the remaining fund in its entirety. However, you are also allowed to transfer the fund to an ARF. Income and gains made by an ARF are tax-exempt; money drawn down from the fund is taxable. In addition, there is an assumption that you will draw down at least 3 percent of the value of the fund each year. (Technically, this is known as an 'imputed distribution'.) You will be taxed on this as if you have withdrawn the 3 percent, so you are best to withdraw it anyway (unless your income, including the imputed distribution, is less than your tax threshold).

A pensioner's ARF fund transfers to his or her next of kin on death. This passes tax free to a spouse and there are certain tax liabilities for inheriting children. Children under twenty-one don't pay income tax on it but they will pay capital acquisition tax (CAT), while children over twenty-one will pay CAT, but not income tax. Others might pay both forms of tax if liable as governed by the normal rules on capital acquisition.

Revenue approves the companies who manage

AMRFs and ARFs. These are usually life assurance companies, banks or specialist investment managers. You should select your investment manager carefully. Remember, you may want them to manage it for a long time and so you must be sure that you will trust them for the long haul. You are allowed, within certain regulations, to switch funds – but remember there is a cost associated with such moves.

Pension time: A decision point

For those with personal pension schemes choosing between buying an annuity and retaining your fund is an important decision. It is something that you should consider carefully and well in advance of retirement. There is no 'correct' decision and it will be affected by other factors such as other income sources and even the state of your health and your potential longevity.

You are probably best advised to take your tax-free lump sum on retirement precisely because it is tax free. The decision between investing your fund in an AMRF or ARF and retaining ownership versus buying an annuity is more difficult. The decision is made a lot easier if you have another income stream. Those who will receive a contributory state pension or other pension benefits may find the fund route more attractive, as they have some security against the possible under-performance of a fund. Get advice, whatever you do, and get it well in advance.

The complexities of tax and pensions

Revenue have complicated regulations governing pensions, their funding and how they are drawn down. Consult an advisor early and find out what regulations govern your particular type of scheme. Seek to maximise the total benefits that will accrue to you on retirement and find out what you should be doing *now* to make sure that you achieve this.

Moving on

Most people change work at least once before retirement. At the same time, the belief underpinning most pension schemes is that employees will stay in the same employment for the entirety of their working lives. Moving on is often a challenging and sometimes difficult time. Moving house, taking on new responsibilities and leaving colleagues and friends behind can easily distract us from pension planning. Personal pension schemes are just that, so they stay with you no matter how often you change jobs. Occupational pensions are more complex.

Those with more than two years' service have a choice about what they can do with their pension entitlements when they leave employment. You can:

- preserve your entitlements in the scheme you are leaving

- transfer them to your new employer's scheme

- transfer them to a policy or contract with a financial institution

Preserving your entitlements means that you will receive a pension benefit relative to the service you've completed in the employment you leave. This increases with the inflation rate or by 4 percent, whichever is less.

You also have the option of transferring your

pension to your new employer should they have an appropriate scheme. You may also move your pension into a PRSA or other personal pension fund.

The National Pensions Framework

The government launched the National Pensions Framework in March 2010. This aimed to address what is sometimes referred to as the 'pensions time bomb'. The document states that close to half of the workforce is not providing for its retirement. In addition, the population is ageing and this will result in fewer workers having to provide for a greater number of pensioners.

The framework document has yet to be converted into legislation and you can expect that it will probably be modified before this happens. Some of the changes will be introduced only when it is prudent to do so; and so it may be some time before the conditions are right. Also, the mechanisms that will allow certain recommendations to come into operation have yet to be worked out. Nevertheless, the framework is a clear indication of the way that the government and policymakers are thinking about providing for your retirement.

There are four broad approaches taken: attempting to reduce the length of time that people spend in retirement; increasing the amount of money invested in pensions; reducing the amount that is paid out; and changes in taxation and regulations relating to pensions.

The first major policy change is that the age at which you will receive your state pension will be set at sixty-six from 2014 and the state pension (transition) is being dropped. The age at which you will receive the state pension will increase to sixty-seven in 2021 and sixty-eight by 2028. This may have significant implications for people who have a pension scheme in place already which is based on the assumption of a retirement age of sixty-five. There may be a need to modify your contract or make extra provisions for any potential shortfall. Remember too that employers usually set an age at which you must retire (normally sixty-five) and so you may have a gap between when you retire and when you qualify for the state pension.

Those entering state employment from the end of 2010 will join a new pension scheme which will have a minimum retirement age of sixty-six, and this will be linked to the state pension age in the future.

The second major change is that everyone in employment aged twenty-two and over, who is not a member of a pension scheme already, will now be automatically enrolled in a new pension scheme. The employer will be required to pay 4 percent of the contribution, the employee will pay 2 percent and the state will contribute another 2 percent. The employee will be able to opt out of the scheme after three months but will be automatically re-enrolled after two years with an option to opt out again. There will be bonuses for those who stay with the scheme for five years without a break in their contributions. There will be a range of pension funds available for those in the scheme, but the state does not guarantee return on investments in the funds. The government will collect this money through the PRSI system and these will be eligible for both Health and PRSI levy relief. This scheme will come into operation when economic conditions allow.

Obviously, the increase in retirement age automatically saves money straight away. There are no definite proposals for changing the way defined contribution payments will be made, but there is an outline of what may happen. It is envisaged that these schemes will have core and non-core benefits. The core benefits will be fixed while the non-core ones will vary according to changes in economic and fund performance.

The government is changing its own defined benefit pension scheme. There will be a single pension scheme for all those who start working in the public sector after 2010. The salary used for the purpose of setting the value of the pension will be based on an average of the earnings over a person's career, rather than their final salary. The government is also considering changing the way that these pensions increase. At present, the value of a retired public servant's pension is normally linked to the salary of their final grade. It therefore increases proportionately with any increase in the salary for that grade. The government intends to break this link and have pensions increase in line with an index (such as the consumer price index).

The tax treatment of pension contributions will change in line with the changes that will come about from the automatic enrolment of people into pension schemes. At present, the rate of tax relief that you receive for your pension contribution is determined by your top rate of tax. Thus, those who earn more receive more tax relief (currently at 41 percent). The state aims to make a contribution to people's pension schemes which will be the equivalent of 33 percent tax relief.

It is also intended to cap the value of a lump sum that you can take tax-free. This will now be set at €200,000; anything greater than this amount is set to be taxed at 20 percent.

There are other proposed changes in pension regulations. All those with defined contribution pensions will now be able to invest their money in an Approved Retirement Fund (ARF) rather than in an annuity. Access to ARFs has been limited until this.

Implications of the framework

One of the most obvious implications of the framework's proposals is for people considering retirement at present who have a large pension pot: people may opt to retire early to avoid the taxation on their lump sum. If you are in this position, then you will have to balance the tax savings against lost earnings etc, making this a very personal choice. Only a relatively small number of people retiring will be affected by this change, as you would need a fund in excess of €800,000 to be able to take out a lump sum in excess of €200,000.

As mentioned earlier, the changes in the age at which one qualifies for the State pension may impact people expecting to retire at an earlier age and who were banking on the State pension as part of their overall pension provisions. This may cause particular difficulties for those who are in their early- to mid-fifties in 2010 and expect to retire at sixty-five.

The changes in tax relief will come into place over the coming years. Those planning to make additional voluntary contributions should explore this option sooner rather than later so that they can benefit from the higher tax relief.

Those with a defined contribution scheme who don't have access to ARFs at present may want to hold off retiring so that they can take advantage of an ARF, rather than an annuity.

The long-term changes in defined benefits schemes will impact greatly on those entering the workforce or changing job in the future. Defined benefit schemes have traditionally given benefits that are both defined and generally of greater value than those from a defined contribution scheme. Changes in these schemes will result in the pensions paid from them being more exposed to market fluctuations and this will increase uncertainty for individual members and pensioners. Those included in these schemes in the future may have to make alternative plans to cover the non-core, risky elements of the schemes. However, the level of uncertainty or risk that pensioners may face in the more distant future will only become evident when the details are fully worked out.

The government's plan to use an average of people's earnings to determine pensions in the public sector will reduce the pensions paid and thus the total pension's budget. This will only begin to have an impact in the long term, but those joining the public service from the end of 2010 onwards will have to evaluate their pension requirements much more carefully. The new approach may punish those who rise up through the civil service ranks when compared with those who join the civil service at higher grades. The linking of the pension to the consumer price index will probably result in smaller pension rises for public servants who retire under this proposed scheme.

Overall, the underlying trends in the framework document indicate that successive governments are likely to pare away benefits for pensioners and those providing for their retirement. It is also evident that responsibility for providing for your golden years will be pushed away from government and employers and towards individuals – with the state providing the very minimum possible.

5

Continuing to Work:
Planning the work/life balance for your golden years

As emphasised already, we may wish to continue working after we reach our retirement age. Retirees are now healthier, fitter and with a greater life expectancy than ever. They also have a greater expectation of what life has to offer people in their later years.

Some people may have made insufficient provisions for their pension and so must continue to work to provide or supplement the money that they need for the life they want. This isn't necessarily a burden if you've enjoyed your working life to date. Others who have enjoyed their work and the social interactions that they've had may want to continue working even though they have sufficient funds to allow them not to. Whatever reason you may have for working after retirement, it's important that you start planning for it properly.

Staying where you are

For some, the choice is obvious – stay in the job you're doing currently. This is particularly easy for those who own their own business or are self employed. Others, though, may not have this option as their employment contract stipulates a mandatory retirement age – usually sixty-five. Certain jobs, for example those in the army or the Gardaí, may have a much earlier mandatory retirement age. There is a mandatory retirement age of sixty-five for specified civil servants, although civil servants who joined after 1 April 2004 have a minimum (that is, they can't retire) retirement age of sixty-five. Private sector companies too may operate mandatory retirement age policies.

There has been a noticeable shift in attitudes to retirement age in recent years. As people live longer and it becomes more difficult to find good recruits, there is an attraction to keeping established employees in an organisation. Expect to find greater opportunities for staying on in employment over the next decades.

Easing out slowly

One attractive way of leaving the world of work is to change from full-time to part-time or temporary working. This allows you to disengage gradually while becoming used to a reduced income and having more time. It offers both financial security and structure. It is also beneficial for an employer, as it makes sure that they continue to have your experience while your replacement grows into the position.

The downside of staying on either as a full-time or part-time employee may be that you are working for less pay. If you work in an organisation with a defined benefit scheme and you qualify for full benefits from it, then you are usually entitled to your full pension at retirement age. Therefore, you may be working for half pay if you continue to work and are not drawing down your pension.

There are other potential problems in staying with the same employer. By virtue of continuing to be there you may be holding a post that a younger colleague wants, and this may create resentment and bad feelings. You also run the risk of being seen as less committed if you work part-time after years of full-time work. The atmosphere at work will change and may be tainted if you overstay your welcome.

Taking another job

One option open to those reaching their later years is following a different career path altogether. We've mentioned some of the preparation you need to do earlier, but it is worth examining the options open to those retiring from employment further.

You should start planning the next phase of your life well in advance of your retirement. Start by making sure that you have the qualifications and skills necessary to pursue your new career. But remember, you'll need more than that to succeed.

Ask yourself some basic questions and list out what you want from the job:

- Do you want full-time or part-time work?

- Do you anticipate being a permanent or casual employee?

- What pay level would you expect?

- How senior of a position are you looking for?

- Are you looking for something local or distant?

- What specifically do you want to get from the work, other than financial reward?

- How long do you intend to work for?

- What size company do you want to work for?

Finding a job after retirement is very much the same as finding one at any other age. One benefit you have is time to prepare. You can start well in advance – perhaps five years before you actually reach the age at which you plan to retire. Don't start planning more than five years ahead though, as it may be unsettling for you in your current employment and may affect your performance and motivation.

If you plan to stay in the same line of work, then start networking with others who are well established in the business long before you plan to retire from your current position. There are obvious moves you should make, such as joining and attending the meetings of business associations and institutes. You may not qualify for full membership, but you may be able to join as an associate, and this will allow you to attend meetings and get copies of newsletters and other industry publications.

Use your contacts to find out what opportunities exist for older people in your sector. Find out how and where they recruit people from and find out what their attitude is to recruiting older people.

You may find that certain recruitment consultants specialise in your sector. You should contact them and find out what they are looking for now and what they are likely to be looking for when you reach retirement age. Check what opportunities are open for contract workers, as you probably won't be interested in permanency.

Try to meet people from your competitors and find out how they operate. You are unlikely to find exactly the same job doing what you did before, so it's good to know what other skills you'll need in a different setting.

You could also be proactive and work to raise your profile. Experience is valuable and you may find that local universities, institutes and colleges may be seeking people to work as temporary lecturers, teachers or trainers. Professional institutes often run evening courses and may be seeking industry specialists to act as teachers or tutors.

Getting involved in your profession's institute or local chamber of commerce will also help raise your profile. Most organisations find it difficult to find people who will join committees, organise meetings or help with administration. Volunteer for these posts. If you're not keen to do this or you don't have the time, then think about putting your name forward to speak at meetings or contribute articles to institute or trade newsletters.

You should also keep abreast of developments in your speciality through the trade and technical publications and websites. Don't confine yourself to Irish sites and publications, but look at international ones, too.

Being your own boss

One dream you might have for retirement may be setting up on your own, and many people start-up in their later years plump for either sole trader status or establishing a limited company. This will allow you to work more flexibly and exploit new opportunities.

Before you do anything, you should consider exactly what sort of business you want to establish. It is easier to operate as a sole trader, but you may have more security and be taken more seriously as a limited company also known as a limited liability company (LLC). Partnerships offer another route – should you want to work with others – while a co-operative may better suit some.

For tax purposes, you are a sole trader as soon as you start working. You may have to register for VAT if your turnover is above certain thresholds (€70,000 for the supply of goods and €35,500 for providing services). You need to be careful about this because the limits are annual, meaning that they are set for income earned in the entire year but if you exceed a quarter of the annual limit in one quarterly period then you need to be registered for and charge VAT. This can affect those who plan to only work for part of the year. You may also wish to register your name with the company's registration office – but this is optional.

Sole traders make tax returns in the normal way. You may need to get help doing your books but the costs for this service are generally lower for a sole trader than for a limited company. A sole trader can only claim for expenses actually incurred, and this on the basis of receipts kept. This may come as a surprise for those who have worked in a company or in the public service where they may claim daily allowances rather than actual expenses or an allowance based on mileage travelled rather than actual petrol expenses.

You can start working as a sole trader at any time. You may find it's possible to carry out some work as a sole trader with another company providing business services to them prior to retiring from your employment. Make sure that there isn't any conflict of interest between the two and that your employer is comfortable with the arrangement.

A sole trader's personal assets are at risk if the business is sued or fails. This is the major problem with that form of business and it is why people often prefer the protection of a limited liability company. A limited liability company is a separate entity from the people who own the company. As such, your liability is limited to your shareholding, normally just a couple of Euros. The major advantage of a limited company is that it protects you from creditors should your business be sued or fail while owing money – as long as you have operated within company regulations and the law.

Limited companies have other advantages, too; for example they are usually regarded as more professional and credible. Potential customers know that a limited company has its books audited annually and this helps to give confidence. People also recognise that it takes effort to establish a company and there is also a continuing commitment to meet revenue and other requirements and this gives a sense of stability and commitment. People responsible for procurement will regards a limited company as more credible and professional. As mentioned already, the methods for claiming expenses are more beneficial for those working in or running a limited company.

On the other hand, a limited company is more formal and has greater reporting requirements. You have to register with the Companies Registration Office and file company accounts with that office at least annually. Limited companies will pay more for auditing their accounts. An accountancy company preparing these will charge considerably more than a bookkeeper would charge for a sole trader. But the expense is necessary, because a company has to prove that it is complying with the relevant legislation.

Owners of limited companies can pay themselves as employees. You must register for tax and PRSI and make regular returns at times set by Revenue. You must do the same for VAT. Your company will also have to pay tax on any profits that it generates.

You can establish a limited company at any time and you may choose to do so in advance of retirement – the same cautions apply as with a sole trader. It is useful to have the basics done before retiring such as appointing directors, registering the company, getting your company seal, getting cards and headed note paper printed, etc.

Setting up as a sole trader is very straightforward. You must register with the revenue commissioners as self employed and you pay tax under the self-assessment system. You may then trade under your own name. Should you wish to use a business name then you must register this with the Companies Register

Office. The office issues a certificate which you must display prominently in your place of business. You will need a certificate of business name to establish a business bank account.

Think carefully about setting up on your own

Starting your own business in your later years may seem attractive – importing wine from southern climes, knitting stylish clothes for the US market or helping companies resolve difficult issues – but there are downsides.

You may incur expenses at the very outset. For example, if you are setting up a manufacturing process, you will need premises. Start-up costs, marketing expenses, utility and communications costs all add up. Staff, if you hire them, will cost you too. Initial capital and running costs are stressful for those who aren't used to dealing with them.

Then there is the pressure of time. You may wish to work at a gentle pace, but working for yourself won't necessarily allow you to. At the start, you may have to take whatever business comes your way. This may mean working long hours to meet strict deadlines. After all, you have to establish your reputation and customers will often expect miracles. Most people running their own businesses work far longer hours than those working for someone else. This can have an impact not just on yourself, but those around you too.

And businesses fail. Small businesses struggle to survive in the first two years and have to work hard to keep going after that. Be prepared to face difficulties or even failure while you work and hope for success. You must ask yourself: do you really want to gamble your lump sum on your business dream?

Preparing to succeed

There are certain steps that you can take to help make sure that your business venture succeeds. For a start, you should enrol for a course in starting your own business before you retire. FÁS is among several state-funded bodies which provide such training. Contact your local enterprise body to find out what they can offer in terms of support. Get training in computers and information technology if you are not already proficient.

Working from home

Those branching out on their own may consider working from home. This is usually a low-cost way of dipping your toe in the commercial waters. Think first about the impact of such a change on your home and those who occupy it. Will a partner who has had a house to his- or herself for a long time be happy to share it with business visitors? What about neighbours? How will they react to your activities? Will there be an impact on parking? What about noise? And so on.

Those planning to run a business from home should keep this in mind whenever they carry out renovations on their home: if you think that you will need a home office at some stage in the future, make sure that any changes that you make to your home take this into account. You need to check practical issues such as client access, plugs for equipment, ventilation if you have a lot of heat generating equipment, etc. You may want to consider building a garden office. Remember too that you have to meet basic health and safety requirements for yourself and for anyone you may employ in your home.

6

Your Home is Your Asset

Your home is likely to be your greatest investment and potentially your best asset. Generally, we buy our home and then invest in it periodically to change it to suit our needs. It's also an asset that must be maintained in our later years. We'll need to keep it warm, dry and as problem-free as possible.

Homeowners should look at their home carefully and long before retiring. You can make changes now that will save money for later. You should also consider your needs in your later years when making any modifications to your home now.

What will your home do for your golden years?

You should examine your home critically at least ten years before you retire or enter your later years. The first decision you have to make is: will this be the home that you want to spend the rest of your life in? For many of us, our home is designed to meet the needs of a growing family rather than a retired couple or individual. Will you find it too large and too costly to run? What about the garden, if you have one? Is it too large or too small for your anticipated needs?

You may decide that you would prefer to live in a smaller house or one in a different location. You should consider making any move in advance of your retirement where possible. This allows you to settle into your new home while you are still in employment and decide what, if any, modifications to it you'll need to make.

The first issue you need to address is the amount and type of space that you'll need in your later years. If you work outside the home then you need to make an allowance for any additional room you'll need when you start spending more time at home. Make allowance for people visiting and staying – including family. You may need additional space for hobbies or new interests. You will need work space for hobbies such as carpentry, pottery and so on.

Look at the costs of running the new home you select. Watch out for management fees in apartment blocks and gated communities. Check the building's energy rating and try to convert that into a real cost of energy. Remember that oil and gas (particularly liquid gas) costs will probably increase significantly in coming years. This is especially the case if you intend to spend more time in your home. You may wish to explore homes that have the capability to be converted to greener heating options. Check other costs too: for example you need to find out when the house was rewired, re-plumbed, had its gutters, roof etc replaced.

You may anticipate profiting from downsizing and

make the move for that reason. The property market is in the doldrums at the time of writing and its crash is a caution for all of us when we're making assumptions about values and gains.

However, it is reasonable to expect some gain. You don't normally pay tax on any gains you make when selling your main or sole residence, because you are entitled to Principal Private Residence (PPR) relief. You can include a garden of up to 0.405 hectares as part of your house for PPR. Using your home for business may affect the PPR relief, as does selling it where it has a 'development value' that is it is being sold for developing. Relief may also be restricted where you have not used the house as your primary home for the full period of ownership. This is important if you have moved into a new home and are still in the process of selling your old one. Normally, Revenue allows you a year to be out of your home before taking away your PPR relief.

There are still other costs associated with moving. For instance, you'll have to pay legal fees for the conveyancing. You should also have a surveyor inspect the house – even if you are buying it without a mortgage – and you'll have to pay their fees, too. The main cost you are likely to encounter is stamp duty. The first €125,000 of the purchase is tax exempt; you'll pay 7 percent on the next €875,000; and 9 percent on the excess over €1 million. Politicians have stated an intention to move away from stamp duty, but it is unlikely that it will ever be abolished totally.

Downsizing costs don't end with the purchase. You will probably have to buy new furniture appropriate to your new home and circumstances. And you may find that you have to carry out some work to modify your new home to your needs.

There may be an advantage in downsizing before retiring, as you can use the excess capital to help provide or boost a pension. For example, you can take out a mortgage when you buy your new home and increase your cash in hand. You benefit from limited mortgage interest relief on the mortgage for the first seven years. Downsizing is a serious step and you need to consider it carefully. You may expect to have a cash surplus if you move from a larger to a smaller home. But be careful, because it probably won't be as much as you expect. Also, carrying out building work in advance of retirement means that you absorb the costs while you are still earning your normal wage. You also have the opportunity to take advantage of any downturns in the market over a longer period.

Your home as an earner

You don't have to sell your house to get it to work on your behalf. Leaving aside re-mortgaging, there are simple ways in which you can make your home earn some income for you.

Revenue allows people who let a room (or rooms) as residential accommodation in the owner's sole or main residence earn up to €10,000 tax free. In addition, you aren't covered by the landlord and tenant legislation. That means you don't have to register with the Private Residential Tenancy Board (PRTB) as a landlord or provide a rent book. You also aren't required to meet any minimum standards and you only need to give reasonable notice. You will still have a legal duty of care, and you should make sure that the room you provide is safe and healthy.

Again, this option is best considered long before you actually put it into operation. For example, those with children may want to modify the children's rooms in a way that gives them the option of letting them at some later stage. You should think about this if you are ever having your house renovated: you may be able to add an en suite bathroom, a separate entrance or even a kitchenette to make it a more attractive rental proposition.

Letting your home is also a good option if you are going to leave it unused for long periods of time. One of the advantages of retirement is that it allows you take longer holidays or other breaks – and out of season. Your home may be attractive as a short-term let either for holidaymakers or people on business visits. You must declare this income for tax purposes, but you may be able to claim certain expenses incurred in the letting such as advertising or management fees.

You may also consider the possibility of dividing your home by adding on an apartment or dividing it into several units. This will require planning permission and you will have to register with the PRTB and follow the landlord and tenancy regulations. You will also have to discuss this with your mortgage provider if you have an outstanding mortgage, as it changes the development and thus changes the basis for that contract. Income that you receive is subject to tax, while relative expenses are allowable against tax.

Taking value from your house

You can draw down some of your home's value as a mortgage. There are specialist mortgages targeted at older people who may find it difficult to raise a mortgage in other ways. These lend you money with no repayments while you are alive and living in your home; but then seek the repayment on your death or when your home is empty for a year or more. The repayments are taken from the proceeds of the sale of the property.

These later-in-life mortgages are normally more expensive than conventional mortgages. They have the advantage of releasing equity – but at a price to your estate. By rolling up the repayments and charging interest on the principal and the added interest, they build up a large charge against the property that is mortgaged. And this is why it is better to explore mortgage borrowing earlier. Taking a mortgage out earlier and at normal rates may be a more effective way of using your property. A lump sum gained earlier may also offer greater investment and income generating prospects than when taken at a later stage.

7

Saving for the Rainy Day

Putting money aside is always wise. Getting into the savings habit shows great maturity. Leaving our savings untouched until later shows restraint and responsibility.

If only we all actually did it!

There are two broad ways of saving – saving in financial institutions and investments in funds, properties, and stocks and shares. The difference between the two is the level of risk involved. The money you put in a bank account should be much more secure than money put into funds (even some guaranteed ones) and the stock market.

The banking crash of 2008 shows that even banks are not completely secure – just look at what happened in Iceland. However, the actions of certain European governments in particular show that the continent's establishment is keen to protect the banking structure. They guaranteed the deposits of savers; share holders and those who invested in funds received no direct government support.

Handling risk

All savings and investments involve an element of risk. You assume that money you put on deposit in a bank is safe. And generally it is.

However, banks do fail and sometimes governments or state institutions let them sink, with losses for their savers and investors. Most governments have a regulatory system in place to make sure that banks and financial institutions don't put their savers' money in jeopardy and that they operate in a responsible way.

Before starting to save, you need to decide on the type of risk you are willing to take. You should make this decision based on the return that you want coupled with the degree to which you can afford to lose the money that you are putting aside. The basic rule is: the greater the return sought, the greater the potential risk involved. If you put your money in a savings account you will receive interest on that investment subject to the bank's rules. If you invest in funds, property or the stock market, then you are putting your money at risk in the hope of a greater return – but there is the possibility that you may lose some or all of the money that you invest.

There isn't a clear distinction between savings and investments. In this book, we'll use 'savings' to refer to money lodged into a bank account paying interest on the money, and without any extra management fees. Savings products should be straightforward, not involved a fund or in need of management to make a return. Bank deposits aren't guaranteed, but in the recent past the Irish government has chosen to provide a limited guarantee for deposits rather than allow a bank to collapse or run into difficulties caused by a run of depositors withdrawing their money. The Government hasn't extended such a guarantee to funds or other investments.

So, how do we deal with risk? The first thing you have to do is be honest with yourself and acknowledge your own feelings about risk. There is little point in making a great return on your money if you spend sleepless nights worrying about it. Even if you are comfortable with uncertainty, you should make sure that you don't bet everything on a single throw of fate's dice.

It's best to look at what you can afford to put aside and then, within that, what you definitely must keep and what you can take a greater risk on. You should also look at when you want the return. The further away the return, the greater the risk you may be taking, and of course you have to put with the peaks and troughs over that times too.

Do I need to save if I have a good pension?

That depends on what you want to do in your retirement, how long you live and what unforeseen events and circumstances occur in between. A pension provides you with a day-to-day income, the lump sum provides a fund to start you off and savings and investments provide the extra money you may need for high-cost and occasional spending that you may encounter in your later years.

The sort of expenses you may consider saving for include:

- replacing your car

- decorating, care and maintenance of properties
- weddings, significant birthdays, anniversary presents and celebrations
- meeting major unexpected costs
- modifications to your home following illness
- care costs (other than those covered by state schemes)
- dream or wish fulfilment

Savings and investments are especially useful for meeting occasional or one-off expenditures. This relative infrequency should determine how you save for them. We'll look at the sorts of savings options open to you and how good behaviours now may make your later years much more enjoyable.

We'll start by looking at savings in banks and financial institutions; later on we'll look at less secure investments.

Banking it

There are three factors that have a major effect on how you save and the way in which you do it:

- the length of time you can lock away your money
- the amount you can put aside
- the rate of interest you earn versus the rate of inflation

Banks want you to save your money for long periods. This allows them to lend it to others – secure in the knowledge that you won't withdraw it until at least the date that you've agreed. They pay you extra interest for this but will punish you if you try to take out your money at an earlier time. On the other hand, you have immediate access to money in a current account or demand account, so you can't expect to earn anything from it and will pay high interest should you go into overdraft.

Most financial institutions offer you the possibility of: investing a lump sum; investing a lump sum with regular savings; regular saving schemes where you agree to set aside a set amount at set times and deposit accounts where you add and take money as you wish. You'll find that financial institutions will offer different combinations of these schemes at different times, and each option needs careful consideration.

Understanding savings and interest

Saving schemes should be straightforward and you must understand exactly what you are agreeing to before entering into any scheme. You should avoid any product that seems overly complex or which has clauses that you can't understand or appear to not make sense.

One of the key points you should pay attention to is the interest rate and the frequency that the institution pays interest to you. Most financial institutions express the interest that they pay as the annual equivalent rate (AER). This is a formula used to express the interest rate in a way that takes account of interest paid and that is added to the capital sum invested. This shows you what the annual interest would be if the interest is compounded and paid at the end of the year rather than monthly, quarterly or whatever time period is used. Interest earned is added to the capital, making the next interest gain slightly larger. Institutions may include interest payments several times a year and thus give a slightly higher AER.

You should make sure that you compare like with like when considering different savings options. Look at both the AER and the restrictions that financial institutions put on the use of your funds. Some savings accounts require that you lodge the money without accessing it for a set period.

Special Term Accounts represent one of the best savings products available at present. Special term accounts give the depositor specified tax-free dividends depending upon the length of time he or she commits to save. There are two kinds available – a medium- and a long-term account. You must invest a lump sum for three years in the medium-term account, and you gain a up to €480 tax-free dividend a year; you must invest the lump sum for five years to gain up to a €635 tax-free dividend a year. But there are restrictions on such accounts:

- You can only have one account (or two in separate names for a couple).

- You also have to leave the money in the account for the full term or incur tax charges if you withdraw early.

- You have to lodge a relatively large amount when opening the account – financial institutions differ on the figure – but it is usually above €3,000.

- You may, in certain schemes, be allowed to add a second instalment of money later.

There are plenty of other savings products available based on either saving a lump sum or depositing regular savings. Investigate all of your options, and you should find that there is a scheme that precisely matches your needs. You don't necessarily need a bank account to save, as both An Post and local credit unions offer a range of savings products, too.

It's good to build a savings habit, if you can afford it, by having a regular deduction from your bank account or pay cheque; you adapt to living without your savings until they mature. And savings do mount. A €100 monthly saving at 2.5 percent interest will amount to over €31,000 after twenty years.

Mixing lump-sum and regular savings also yields significant benefits, especially if you put the lump sum into savings earlier rather than later. For example, if you were to invest a €5,000 lump sum at the start of the example given in the previous paragraph, then the final value of your savings will be close to €40,000.

Planning your savings

There are a few basic things to do when planning your savings. Firstly, make a realistic evaluation of what you can save over the period that you want to save for. Allow for occasional extra demands on your money, such as Christmas and other family occasions. You should visit all of the financial institutions either in person or online and compare the different offerings available.

Don't make decisions on the spot. Companies will put you under pressure to start a contract now. Don't. Even special offers that seem too good to be true will probably be available from some other provider.

When locking your money away, take into account the likely impact of inflation. Remember: the longer you put your money away the more likely it is to pass through a period of high inflation, which may eat away at much of your savings' value. In early 2010, we are passing through a deflationary period, so money that you have put aside is gaining in its buying power. But this won't last. You must take account of the time value of money that is how your money retains its real value over a prolonged time period and you should reduce any gains by what you estimate inflation will be. Check out banks' web pages, where you'll find calculators that estimate your savings' growth based on how much you put aside each month. These will show you how you can vary your savings to meet a definite target. Remember that inflation is not uniform – some prices continue to fall even while others are rising. The cost of housing can have a disproportionate impact on inflation during periods of high interest rates (for those who own their home, this element of inflation is less important). Overall, it is probably best not to lock away too much money for anything more than five years, as it is impossible to predict inflation and interest rates beyond that time.

Those who have grown children and are no longer supporting them might think about putting the money that they once paid for their upbringing into savings and pensions. The same holds true for mortgage repayments – if you've finished making mortgage repayments, why not divert some of that amount into savings? Equally, if you get an increase in pay at work, could you put a portion into savings? This is especially relevant for those who receive a lump sum in back pay – this could make an ideal down payment for starting a savings plan.

Look at your long-term needs and try to estimate what you'll need money for. Remember that those with an adequate pension may be able to continue saving if they need to – even if it is at a reduced rate. This will help reduce the burden of saving in your working life. You should target your savings to deliver the outcome you want at approximately the time that you expect to use the money. For example, if you change your car every five years then it is easy to calculate your needs for this. However, it's harder to plan for home repairs resulting from storms, weather damage or other unexpected spending. It is best therefore to keep some money in readily-accessible accounts to avoid unnecessary borrowing.

You should also watch your current accounts and credit cards and make sure that you are maximising the benefit that they deliver to you. There is little point in saving if you are paying far more in interest on a credit card or overdraft fees. There are current accounts too that offer some interest or free banking if you keep your balance over a certain limit. The gain is minor, but if it includes free or reduced banking fees then it may be worthwhile availing of these.

8

Playing the Market:
Gold for your golden years?

Few of us will ever forget the shock and emotion on
the faces of the pensioners who attended the annual
general meetings of Irish financial institutions after
the crash of 2008. For many of them, the shares
they bought were supposed to be a safe bet and the
annual dividend had become a major part of their income for their later years. Suddenly and calamitously,
their security disappeared.

There is a lesson in this for everyone in their pre-
retirement years. Shares, no matter how sound the
company they're in, are a risk. And the first rule of
investment is to spread your risk. The second rule is
to not invest anything that you can't afford to lose.

There is a mystique surrounding stock market
investing, fuelled by images of those who have made
fortunes on rising markets. Most people who invest
in the market come out with somewhat more than
they would have had they put their money into long-

term savings. And they usually do this by spreading their investments across funds and/or shares.

Investing for your retirement

You need to keep sight of your goals when investing for your later years. There is a danger of getting mesmerised by the investment process itself and following fads or overly risky options. You have to focus.

You can invest in the stock market in different ways. However, there are two core ways of doing so: by putting your money into a fund managed by someone else, who invests it over a range of shares or equivalent of shares; or by buying shares directly.

Investing in funds perhaps lacks the excitement of the stock market trading floor, but it has the advantage of avoiding the most severe losses that can sweep across the markets.

Trusting in funds

There is an abundance of jargon used about investing and investments. Most of it attempts to make things sound more complicated than they really are. When you invest in a fund, your money is pooled with money invested by others and used to buy assets that have the capability of giving a return on the investment. Fund investors then together share the gains and suffer the losses that the fund experiences.

A fund may also include a life assurance policy for the investor. This allows life assurance companies to market these investment products to investors under their licence or appropriate authorisation from the financial regulator.

Banks, building societies, life assurance companies, brokers and other financial institutions operate investment funds. Such an institution has specialist fund managers charged with managing the funds who will usually charge a management fee. The quality of the investment managers is highly important when choosing a fund to invest in. You should also consider the depth of fund management capability that the managing institution possesses, as fund managers move regularly from company to company. You'll get an idea of the depth of expertise in a company from the number and range of funds that it offers. This is not an infallible guide, though, and you should check the experience and number of people involved in managing a fund before entrusting your money to it.

Funds invest in a range of things anywhere in the world. They can buy stocks, government or company bonds, property, or anything that is likely to grow in value. Funds may specialise in a specific sector or region, or it may be defined in terms of the level of security offered. Funds can be for a specific period or continue indefinitely although they may be combined with another fund at a later stage or renamed.

You are allocated 'units' when you invest in a fund. These correspond to your share of that fund. Part of your investment may be taken by the financial institution at the start as a management fee. This is usually around 5 percent of your investment. Institutions often have special offers when starting a fund – such as waiving or reducing the joining fee for early entrants – keep an eye out for these. Funds can be open ended – meaning that as more people invest, the fund adds more units. Other funds have a set number of units.

Some funds are guaranteed and invest in, among other things, government bonds or other very secure products. The guarantee normally applies to your initial capital rather than the growth. You should be given a description of the type and breakdown of the investments in any fund before you invest. Most of these are available on the managing companies' websites should you wish to compare one with another.

There is a progression in the level of risk take you can take when investing in funds. This runs from the guaranteed ones through to funds that seek high rates of growth by investing in more volatile shares and options. Generally, the fund name or description will give an indication of the level of risk involved. A 'cautiously managed' fund means that the managers follow a conservative investment strategy, usually with an emphasis on bonds. 'Aggressively managed' means that the fund contains riskier investments.

Knowing your funds

Fund Type	Where it Invests
Money market	short-term bonds from governments or other very secure institutions giving a set, definite return
Fixed income	government and corporate bonds
Equity	stocks and shares
Property	commercial, retail and residential properties (usually apartment developments)
Balanced	a mix of equity and fixed-income securities

(table continued)

International	equities and fixed-income securities spread across a number of countries
Specialist	concentrating on a particular country (e.g. the US), region (e.g. Asia) or industrial sector (e.g. pharmaceuticals)
Ethical	equities or other securities in businesses meeting set ethical criteria (e.g. green energy or fair trade)
Tracker	a mix of saving deposit and investments with the investments chosen to match a particular index, such as the stock exchange index
With profits	pooled investment fund, usually with a financial institution, where a proportion of any gain is kept back to smooth out later losses

You should be clear about the risks you are taking when investing in funds. There are certain factors to examine:

- **Geographic** – mainly political or social

- **Currency** – investments made in currencies other than euro may be at risk should that currency decline

- **Credit** – those who issue bonds may not be able to repay it when it becomes due

- **Inflation and interest rates** – inflation can wipe out gains while interest rates may decline and thus pay less on funds deposited

- **Liquidity** – fund can't sell or has to discount an asset when investors seek their money

- **Market** – the ups and downs of the stock market

When you look at risk, you should pay attention to your age and when you want to take your money from your investment. If you are investing for a long-off retirement you may decide to follow a riskier option, as you'd have time to recover should something go wrong; if you want a return in the next ten years, then you should look at more secure options with some form of guarantee. Most companies offering investment funds allow you to switch from one fund to another, usually for either a small or no fee. This makes it easier to rebalance your investments as you approach retirement or your target encashment date.

You should find out the charges associated with any fund; its encashment policy and any related charges; its proposed investment strategy and its advice on the suitability of a fund for your particular needs. It is also worth looking a company's record in fund management. Examine all of their funds, but especially those that have a similar investment mix to those you are considering. Sales people will emphasise their best-performing funds, but you need to get an idea of a company's overall performance. Excellent results in a specialist fund concentrating on pharmaceuticals are of little relevance if you plan to put your money into a property fund.

Always take your time when examining funds and take documents away with you to study at your leisure. Read the prospectus carefully and make sure that you are clear about tax treatment and charges before you sign anything. Never sign if you aren't clear about something and don't be afraid to get independent advice if you have any doubts.

Investing directly in shares

Playing the stock market fascinates many. Its mystique may dazzle the unwary. It is now easier than ever to buy and sell shares. However, the recent crash in the world's stock markets shows that it's easy to lose your investment, too.

You come to own a small part of a company when you buy a share in it. We will only deal with companies whose shares are listed on a stock exchange rather than private companies, whose shares are not listed. The price of a share can rise or fall depending on how well the company performs and how the market is performing generally. A share delivers value in two ways: through a rise in the share price or a dividend paid at regular intervals. Shares increase in value when the market believes that they will become more valuable in the future. The dividend is a share of the company's surplus (or 'profit') paid to shareholders relative to the number of shares that they own. Companies don't necessarily pay a dividend each year – even when they make a profit. This is because profits may be used to build up the company, which should result in a long-term increase in its share price.

You buy shares through a stockbroker or your bank. Brokers offer different services depending upon your needs. Execution-only services mean that the broker buys shares on your behalf without offering advice. A broker may also advise you on shares to buy or sell (advisory service) or the broker may act on your behalf within certain limits agreed with you (discretionary service).

Stockbrokers charge fees depending on the service that they provide you with and a commission when they buy or sell shares on your behalf. This means that you incur costs on every transaction, so you have to balance the costs you'll incur against the potential gain. (You will normally pay higher charges if you are investing less than €15,000.) You'll often find that your broker charges a minimum commission on transactions. Remember, a broker gains every time you change your portfolio.

It is possible to trade online through online trading companies. These companies charge lower fees, but obviously come with a different range and depth of service. There are other investment vehicles available online, such as gambling on shares rising or falling. Online trading is less secure than dealing directly with a broker and although it costs less it means that the investor is on their own and takes responsibility for losses and gains. You can avail of online trading services from reputable stock brokers. You will also find training in online dealing on the internet. Those unfamiliar with the stock market or the internet should be very wary of plunging into online trading.

Stockbrokers also offer a product called an exchange-traded fund (ETF), which is traded in the same way as a share. These track a basket of shares or a share index. They allow you to invest in a greater spread of shares across the market and can involve large international companies. Fees are usually lower for ETFs.

New investors sometimes enter the world of stocks and shares through investment clubs. These may take a variety of forms depending on the make-up, wealth and interests of the group. You may benefit from these in that you'll get advice from others and get better value through pooling your funds. But there is a difficulty in that the investment club members are usually amateurs, and therefore the soundness of the advice given or inferred may be questionable.

All share-dealing involves risk and so you should only invest money that you can afford to lose. You pay stamp duty of 1 percent on shares registered in Ireland and 0.5 percent on UK ones when you buy them. When you sell shares, you must pay tax on the dividends that you may receive, and you pay capital gains tax on profits you make above €1,270 in any tax year.

You are taking a great risk if you are planning to depend upon share income as a major portion of your retirement income. You should look to reduce such exposure and move the bulk of your money into more secure products long before your retirement date.

9

Property as an Investment

It may seem like a joke to include property as an investment prospect after the crash in the late noughties. But like any asset, property in the right place and at the right cost can yield a good return.

There is a one significant difference between property and shares: property is permanent. For many, the fact you can see and feel it makes property more 'real' and therefore a more realistic investment. Buying an investment property is very different than buying your own home. But if you have bought your own home then you'll have developed some of the skills that you need for this kind of investment.

Property investment could be especially suitable for those planning their retirement. For example, you can calculate the length of a mortgage for an investment property so that it runs out on or before your retirement date. Such that, if you planned to rent out the property, the rental income would become part of your pension or the sale of the property gives you a lump sum to invest or enjoy.

We've also mentioned pension mortgages earlier, and some of you may wish to explore setting up a specific pension based on property. You'll need expert legal and financial advice to construct this complicated option, so in this section we'll concentrate on direct property investment rather than that through another financial mechanism.

Buying to let

There are a number of key decisions to make when you're buying a property to let as an investment. There's the type of property – commercial, retail or residential? Do you plan to self build or buy a finished item? Are you hoping to gain mainly from the growth in the property's value or from the rental income? Maintenance, security and how rentable the property is all come into play too. And, of course, there's location – location is the most important factor, from the initial cost of the investment, through to the rent you can get for it and the potential resale value later.

Individuals investing in commercial properties often do so as part of a syndicate or group where each person puts in a certain amount of money to create a pot sufficient to buy a large commercial property. Examine such options from the perspective of liquidity, value and the marketplace.

Liquidity refers to the ease with which you can extract your money should you need it for something else. The problem is that at the early stage, particularly if you are involved in a development that's still being built, it may be very hard to get your money back in a hurry. And even when the property is built and let, then you are dependent on someone else buying out your share to realise your capital.

Value becomes more complex when there is a group of investors involved. You won't all want the same from the development. You need to be sure that the property bought meets *your* needs, especially your retirement planning needs. 'Groupthink' can sometimes be a problem with a group of enthusiastic property investors: they may pay over the price and thus reduce the return. You must look at the likely lifetime of the project to ensure that it doesn't need recapitalisation at a time when you want your money for enjoying your golden years.

You can have little idea of what the market for commercial property will be when you come to cash in your investment. Unfortunately, it's difficult to predict what will happen over the years in between. The commercial and retail markets experience peaks and troughs reflecting international and national movements – probably more so than the residential sector.

Residential properties: An easier option

This is a bad time to buy to let in Ireland. There is an over-supply of properties on the market and a lack of finance to buy it. It is difficult to predict when or if the market will start to grow again and renting become an attractive option for landlords. However, you can buy properties for a lot less now than in the past decade and there is the prospect of getting an increased return should the market come back.

Buying a residential property to let may involve a lot of effort but it has the possibility of giving a long-term, manageable return. As with everything else, property investment requires research, taking advice and avoiding the obvious pitfalls.

Buying to let has special attractions as part of a retirement planning package. One is that you can include the property or properties bought as part of your overall life planning. Should you have children away from home at college then you may think about buying an apartment that they can use. You can then let this when they vacate it. You may even be able to get some extra income if your student child is willing to share it with friends or roommates during their college years.

But there are other life-plan uses for a buy-to-let property. For example, you may wish to move to a smaller home in your later years. Why not buy the smaller property long before you need it? This allows you the possibility of earning rent while you work and before you actually want to live in it.

Funding your investment

It's hard to raise a loan for property in Ireland right now. It may be even harder to raise a mortgage for a property for renting, whether it's commercial, retail or residential, until the market re-establishes itself. You pay more for a commercial mortgage than for a home mortgage, and you may face further restrictions on the amount that you may borrow, the acceptable state of repair, etc.

You need to have some capital yourself when buying. If you are cash-rich at present then you should be able to benefit from the greatly reduced prices available in the marketplace.

Costs and other expenses

You'll encounter additional costs when purchasing for letting. You'll pay stamp duty in Ireland when you purchase here, and you also face the prospect of property tax – just introduced for additional residential properties in Ireland and likely to increase over the life of your investment. You will have to register as a landlord, obey the laws governing letting and pay tax on your income after you've deducted allowable expenses.

You will also have to repair and maintain your property over the years. It will have to be furnished, painted, repaired etc. You may also have to pay service charges if the property is in a private development with a management company. It is important to find out exactly what these charges are – especially if the building is only partly occupied or if there is work awaiting completion.

Remember too that you'll pay capital gains tax when you sell the property.

Buying abroad

Buying property abroad for letting either as a holiday home or for a full-time let is a relatively new phenomenon for Irish people. During the boom, Irish people bought across Europe, the Middle East, the United States, the Far East and China. Unfortunately, some of the properties bought during this splurge proved not to exist or to be very poor investment value. This experience has tarnished overseas property investment and may have frightened off prospective Irish investors.

But this may be an over-reaction. There is good value and solid income available internationally if you know where to look and have the time and patience to find it – especially when coupled with the relatively dreary outlook for the Irish market.

Buying overseas – as part of planning for your later years – requires a bucket-load of common sense and a sharp eye for chancers. Most of the same cautions apply to buying internationally as to buying at home.

You have the option of working through agencies specialising in overseas properties or doing the footwork yourself. You should check out any agency you deal with and try to get a referral from someone who has used its services and is happy with the outcome.

You should also analyse the purchasing risk for any area that you are considering. Look at figures for growth – both in population and the economy over the past decade. There are parts of continental Europe, for example, where the population is declining rapidly. Property prices tend to follow suit. Once you've identified the country and region that you are willing to invest in, you can choose your property.

You should make sure that you visit prospective properties before you agree to buy anything. It is naïve in the extreme to buy from plans or to accept the recommendation of an interested agent based in Ireland. Visit the property privately, away from the salesperson. Walk around the block and get a sense of what the area is like. You should visit other estate agents in local towns and get a sense of what is on offer. Try to approach the developer independently and find out what the property would cost if you bought it directly. You may be very surprised at the agent's mark-up: agents sometimes charge on the double – to the seller and the buyer.

Check too for any other management, parking or maintenance fees associated with the property before you make the final decision to buy.

Get local advice if you can – find and contact Irish or British people living locally who may be able to help you. They may tell you what they have paid; know about the rental market and the ups and downs of a locality. Never buy without inspecting and comparing properties. Be careful of selling techniques such as leaseback or guaranteed income offers; Irish investors have been burnt by such schemes in the past.

Make sure that you get local independent legal and technical advice. You need to understand local risks and laws. For example, parts of Bulgaria are prone to severe earthquakes – did Irish people who have invested in that region take account of this and have an appropriate survey conducted before purchasing? Take a long-term perspective too – if you are buying a ski property, then how sure are you that the ski slopes will survive global warming? You should also explore local plans, particularly regional development plans, to make sure that the development is legal and/or there are no major projects planned that will adversely affect your prospective property's value.

You should make sure that you understand the law where you are buying and that you engage a competent lawyer and find out what service they provide. Lawyers in different countries provide different services which may not match those provided by solicitors in Ireland. You also need to find out what the law is concerning letting and the potential legal pitfalls. Does a tenant gain rights over the property, and what are they?

Overseas financing

It is possible to borrow abroad, and in some countries with more attractive terms than are available in Ireland. For example, in some countries you can avail of mortgages with fixed interest rates for the full term of the mortgage. This is especially useful if you plan to use part of your pension for the repayments in the latter stages of the mortgage. Always calculate what would happen if you were unable to let your property for a prolonged period.

Income and outgoings

There are overseas agents who offer letting and maintenance services. Check the fees and how they are calculated. Agents specialise in different parts of the market and some will concentrate on holiday or short-term lettings while others focus on the long-term. Those letting for the short-term are more likely to take a very high percentage (20%) of the overall rental income. You should also find if those providing holiday letting services shut up shop out of season. Holiday rental income plummets off season but you may hope to get some income during that time and therefore you want the agent to be working on your behalf. Talk to other customers and find out how happy they are with the services provided. Make sure too that you understand any maintenance services provided and how you will be charged for. In summary, short-term letting yields much higher rents, but you incur more agency and related fees and you run the risk of your property being empty for long periods. Long-term letting may give the tenant greater rights, with lower rental yield.

You should have the rent paid directly into your own account – set up an expatriate account with a bank in that country.

Expect to pay annual property and income tax overseas. You will be able to offset this against income tax in Ireland if there is a reciprocal arrangement. You may also have to pay extra taxes when you are selling overseas – especially if you are selling within a short time of purchasing.

10

Moving Away

Travelling or living abroad is often put forward as part of the 'ideal retirement'. Advertisements for pension schemes feature couples strolling on Mediterranean beaches or slipping into a beachside *taverna* for an evening meal while sitting gazing over a flat, calm sea bathed in the light of the evening sun. You'll only achieve the dream of a golden years paradise if you start working on it long before you reach them. You should read the section on buying property for investment in conjunction with this section.

Moving house is often part of people's retirement dreams; and it's one with significant financial implications. You may wish to change where you are living in Ireland – moving from the city to a country village for example – but the move is still very significant. On the other hand, you may wish to go abroad, change continent even, and this will involve considerable financial and lifestyle change.

Changing your home and moving to a very different environment is a major event and something that you shouldn't take lightly. It will impact on your finances and the plans you make long before you actually make the move.

There's plenty of anecdotal evidence to suggest that moving in your later years to an area that you don't know and where you have no connections can be difficult. Without the familiar social supports, life may become more stressful and less enjoyable. This is as likely to happen to someone who relocates within Ireland as it is for someone who goes abroad. Obviously, moving within your own neighbourhood is much less traumatic.

Start exploring your new locations years or more before you intend to move. Make a list based around the following:

- City, town, village or rural location

- New property or older

- With or without a garden

- Seaside, lakeside, coastal, inland, hills or mountains

- Access: bus, trains, airports, roads and lanes

- Social mix: other retirees

- Activities in the area during daytime, night-time, summer and winter

- Amenities: restaurants, shops, pubs, cafes and services such as cleaners, repair services and painters

- Medical care: doctors, dentists, pharmacies, hospitals

- Entertainment, culture and sport: cinemas, theatres, libraries, festivals, gyms, sports grounds etc

- Security: crime levels and policing

- Walking distances to and from amenities, lighting and security along the route

- Walks, running tracks, cycling routes and the general safety of these

- Communications services: phones, broadband internet, terrestrial, cable or satellite TV or radio

- Climate: average seasonal temperatures, precipitation and predictability of climate and its stability

- Cost of living and availability of products and services you may like to use

- Costs such as local taxes, water charges, estate management company charges

- Natural factors such as risk of drought, flooding, landslides, seismic activity other natural disasters

Renting or buying a new home involves making compromises on some of these points in order to gain on others. One key consideration for those moving abroad to holiday-type destinations is the quality of life during the off-season. Some sun destinations almost close down during the winter, as do some rural villages. The best approach is to try out the location in both summer and winter to make sure that it's pleasant in both.

I would suggest that, if you can, you buy a holiday home in your chosen location as long before you plan the move as possible. This gives you a chance to find out if you really do like the life there. It also means that you've established a presence there; and if you don't like what you have or where you are, then you have an asset to sell that should have kept pace with the local market.

Of course, a holiday house also offers the possibility of earning rental income should you choose to let it when you aren't using it. As with all lettings, make sure that you choose your tenants and leases carefully.

Preparing to relocate

There is a big difference between holidaying in an area and living there for a prolonged period. Preparing well in advance will save you money and improve the quality of your experience abroad. A simple thing you can do, for example, is to enrol in language classes with a local evening school or college. Learning a language over a long period is cheaper and more effective than taking a crash course just before you plan to move. Public servants in particular may be able to take advantage of free language training programmes and they may have the opportunity to travel overseas either for training or work.

You will get a real feel for a country if you work or spend a long time in it. You should make your employer aware of your interest in working in a specific region or market. Check for other opportunities that may present themselves, such as leaves of absence, training abroad or secondment to another office or supplier.

A more radical option may be to find a job with operations in or a commitment to the market that you are interested in.

Networking with those with an interest in the country that you want to relocate to is a good way of finding out about how the country operates and the opportunities available there. There are business or friendship associations for most countries popular with Irish travellers and businesspeople; countries with closer ties have cultural institutes in Ireland. Volunteering for committees and tasks will raise your profile and bring you to the attention of those that are also committed to developing contacts. Chambers of commerce have contact networks with sister organisations overseas and you can use these if you want to explore business opportunities abroad.

Rent or buy?

Once you've identified your location you need to decide whether you want to buy or rent there. If you are already retired or are very close to retirement when making the move, I recommend that you rent first to find out if you like the region in general and your location in particular. It is important to test the water before plunging in. Remember too that tenants have greater rights in many European countries, so long-term renting is a practical and relatively secure option there. An alternative approach open to retirees is to rent a holiday home off-season for the six months from October to March – this will show you what the place is like at a quieter time.

Buying a home abroad

Buying a property abroad or somewhere else in Ireland should be treated with the same seriousness as buying at home. Where possible, I advise that you buy the property as long before retirement as you possibly can. Early buying gives you a longer period of time to structure your financing in a way that is more favourable to you and may leave you with fewer worries at the time. You can renovate a property more cost-effectively if you have more time and you can furnish it gradually with less expense. On the other hand, you may be planning to sell your current home and buy elsewhere on retirement. In such a case, I recommend a period of renting – if that is possible.

Buying a home abroad may differ significantly from doing the same in Ireland. The laws, languages, roles of professionals and processes may be unfamiliar. Unless you are fluent in the local language, you will need a translator to help you through the process. The *notaire* in France, for example, is not the same as a solicitor in Ireland. He or she acts on behalf of the state to make sure that both buyer and seller adhere to French law – rather than your behalf – and so you need additional advice. There are some Irish-based lawyers who can help guide you through the process of buying overseas and you should be guided by their advice.

It is difficult to anticipate all of your needs for your later years – especially when you may be planning twenty years in advance. You should make sure that you build additional security into your choice of overseas destination. For example, ensure that you have multiple travel options between your Irish base and your chosen location if you plan to commute between the two. Flights with regular airlines, as opposed to budget ones, will be a significant burden if you will be paying for them out of a pension.

There are certain factors that will indicate whether an area is prospering and has good long-term prospects. You can check school enrolment in the area you are interested in: if it's increasing, then that may suggest a growing population and therefore guarantee services and property values. An ageing population with declining numbers will probably be accompanied by a drop in services with an impact on property values.

Bi-locating

A favoured option for many retirees is to move between two or more different locations in their retirement. You may want to keep a home base but live abroad for an extended time each year. There are options that allow you to achieve this relatively inexpensively.

If you have a home in Ireland, then you may be able to let it as a short-term let while you are overseas. Think about this option should you ever be renovating or adapting your home in the decades prior to your retirement. Consider what potential tenants will look for in your house, such as extra storage space and additional bathrooms to allow people who are not related to share. You should also look at modifying it so that you have a secure storeroom or other safe place for your valuable possessions. Think too about fitting a safe for small valuables that you may want to leave behind.

You don't necessarily have to own a house for your overseas leg. I've met people living on their houseboat on canals in the south of France while their homes are let in Ireland. Others I've met work as caretakers for holiday apartments in Spain during the winter. You should start establishing links that will allow you set up such arrangements well in advance.

Maintaining two houses means a significant increase in your outgoings. You'll probably have to pay taxes in both countries. You will have double the standing charges for your utilities and, should you maintain a car in both, then you'll see these costs double, too. You'll also have to allow for insurance for two properties and, if you let one or the other, you may have to pay an additional premium.

In addition, you may have to register with the police or apply for a temporary residence visa should you plan to remain in one country for an extended stay. You should check these regulations well in advance of committing to a specific country.

Money abroad

You continue to be entitled to the state contributory pension if you move abroad after retirement; but you have to be resident in Ireland to qualify for the non-contributory pension. You don't have to spend a specific time in Ireland in any one year to be an ordinary resident. Those with pensions should have them paid into an account that is easily accessible and allows you to transfer money overseas for reasonable fees.

Also, you'll have to register for tax wherever you move should you take a full- or part-time job. Pay rates may be substantially lower in other countries, so be cautious when working out your budget. Taxes and other employment charges vary significantly from country to country and you can't anticipate receiving the same abroad as you would in Ireland. You may build up social welfare and employment rights in your adopted country should you stay in employment for a reasonable length of time.

You may also have to budget for long-term private medical insurance if you spend over half a year abroad. Most policies, including those of companies such as VHI or Aviva, only cover you for 180 days overseas. You will qualify for treatment within the EU subject to certain regulations, but you should anticipate that you will have to pay a significant extra premium if you haven't got the proper health coverage.

11

Taking Care of Others

We've concentrated on planning for your golden years, but you may also want to plan for others close to you; and you'll want to make sure that you don't leave a financial mess behind you when you do finally pass away. Most of us are also keen to make sure that whatever we leave behind goes where we want it to – and not to the Revenue.

Start with the most obvious. Anyone with assets should make sure that they make a will setting out what they want to happen to their worldly goods. If you haven't – do it immediately. List your assets: possessions, property, investments and bank accounts. Don't forget any life assurance policies that you have or any pension fund you've established. Decide who you would like to benefit from what you leave behind (your estate). Then you must decide how you would like to distribute your estate. You must also get two people to agree to act as your executors. Once you've done this, contact a solicitor and get professional legal advice on drawing up a will.

No matter what else, you should make sure that you have a will in place – even if this is only an interim one. You can modify this at a later date, when you've decided exactly how you want to distribute your assets and care for those depending upon you.

Capital Gains Tax (CGT) and Capital Acquisitions Tax (CAT) (including inheritance/gift taxes) are the two taxes that you have to watch. CGT refers to any profit you make from, for example, selling an asset other than the family home; CAT is levied on any capital you acquire through, for example, a gift or inheritance (gift and inheritance taxes are parts of CAT). The person receiving the gift is liable for the tax and it is further complicated by having different rates depending on when the gift was given. It is fair to speculate that these taxes will change further in the near future, and so readers planning for the long-term should monitor them very closely.

The earlier you start transferring assets, the better it may be from a tax perspective. You may have promised something to a child or relative and want to give it to them so that they can get the maximum benefit from it earlier rather than later. You may also wish to shift the responsibility for the asset to the person who will receive it eventually. Whatever your reason, you should develop a clear plan and consult those who will be affected by the decision.

Remember that it is the recipient who benefits from your good tax planning, and you don't want to give up something that you personally still need or want.

You can give gifts to others up to a certain level without them incurring any tax liability. (The same amounts apply to inheritance.) The levels are as follows:

Year	Group A: child or foster child*, minor child of deceased child (child to parent for inheritance tax only)	Group B: parent, brother, sister, niece, nephew, grand-child, minor child of a deceased child, lineal descendent other than child	Relationship other than A or B
On or after 8 April 2009	€434,000	€43,400	€21,700
1 January 2009 to 7 April 2009	€542,544	€54,254	€27,127
2008	€521,208	€52,121	€26,060
2007	€496,824	€49,682	€24,841

*A foster child must have been cared for, maintained by and lived with you for five successive years before the age of eighteen years.

The first €3,000 of a gift from any one person is exempt from gift tax; but that exemption doesn't apply for an inheritance. The tax, gift or inheritance, is currently 25 percent above the threshold shown in the table above. Gift tax doesn't apply to a gift from one spouse to another or where it is given for the medical expenses of a person who is permanently incapacitated because of physical or mental illness. There are other exclusions, but these are not relevant to planning your later years.

Transferring your home

There are tax efficient ways of transferring your home, business or farm to someone close to you.

Parents often wish to pass on their home (the principal private residence) to a child or a homeowner may want to give it to another who has lived with them for a long time. You can now do so without the recipient being liable for gift tax – within certain strict conditions. The person who receives the house must have lived there as his or her only or main residence for the three years prior to the transfer. However, not everyone has lived in the same house for three years. If, for example, you change home within the three years prior to when you want to transfer ownership, you can still do so without tax liability as long as the recipient has fulfilled the living conditions in the first home. They must have lived in the house for three of the last four years prior to the gift.

The recipient can't be the part or outright owner of any other house at the time the gift is made. They must also stay in the house as their main or only residence for a further six years after receiving the gift to avoid inheritance tax. There are exceptions to the six-year rule – it doesn't apply if the person is over fifty-five years of age. Again, the recipient can move house as long as the second property replaces the first and the recipient completes the remainder of the six years in the new one. The recipient won't have to pay gift tax if they are unable to complete the six years' residency due to a need for long-term medical care in hospital or a nursing home. The exemption also remains where the person has to work overseas or where their employer requires them to move.

Handing over your house to someone else is a serious move and you need to consider it and plan carefully. You should get advice from a solicitor and a tax advisor to make sure that everything is legal and tax efficient. Obviously, you will no longer own what was your home and so cannot use it as security for borrowing or as a possible source of income in your later years. You are presuming that relationships will remain amicable should you plan to remain in your home after giving it away. This has been the cause of bitter disputes in the past and will doubtless continue to be so for some in the future.

You can also give a child a site for a house without incurring capital gains tax liability as long as it is for their own home. (Note: broadly the same conditions apply to a person inheriting a house in which he or she has lived as described for gift tax.)

Passing on the business or farm

There are different tax regulations governing the transfer of a farm or family business to another, depending upon the relationship involved and the age of the individual disposing of the assets. There is a special retirement relief from CGT for people aged fifty-five years or older, and transfers between spouses are not subject to CGT.

If you have owned a business for more than ten years and you are over fifty-five years old, you can sell it to your child (or a niece or nephew who has worked in the business for the previous five years) without being liable for CGT. There is no limit on the value of the business being transferred. Where the asset is disposed of in the form of shares in a family business, then the person disposing of the shares must have been a working director for ten years (five of these must have been as a full-time, working director). The recipient must hold onto the assets for six years; if they are disposed of before that time then you are liable for CGT on the benefit gained. Therefore, you need to be sure that the relative taking over the business is doing so for the long term.

You may simply want to give your asset to your child rather than charging them for it. In this case they can benefit from a major concession on acquisition tax: they are allowed to write down the value of the assets transferred by 90 percent. For example, if a business is valued at €1 million, then for CAT purposes the value is €100,000 and the recipient will pay CAT tax at 25 percent of that sum – €25,000.

There are restrictions on this benefit and these are similar in many respects to those applying to the CAT in other acquisitions. You must have owned the business for five years before disposing of it, and the person receiving the assets must keep them for six years or risk having the tax clawed back. Assets that can be included in this scheme are wide-ranging and can include land and machinery owned by the person giving the gift, if they are used by the company. Businesses whose sole activity is financial or land dealing cannot take advantage of this concession.

Transferring a farm is very similar to transferring a business. The same discounting of the value applies – 90 percent. There is a very broad view taken of the assets included as part of the farm and it may include money earmarked for investment in farm property within two years. The person receiving the farm only has to be a 'farmer' in the broadest meaning of the word. The sole requirement is that a minimum 80 percent of his or her assets must be farm ones. I've known of people simply transferring their other assets into their spouse's name to ensure that their assets were less than the legal threshold.

People benefiting from your generosity may still pay some tax. Even your children may have to pay tax for assets that don't benefit from a concession. You can put an assurance policy in place to meet this expense and the payments from insurance or assurance policies are exempt from CAT.

The taxes on transferring your wealth mean that you should plan gifts and bequests carefully. Decide how and when you want to dispose of your assets and then work out how you can match these against what is allowable under the tax laws.

Providing for a dependent with a disability

For people planning for their later years, their main concern may be providing for an adult child or close relative with disability. This is a complex area which needs careful consideration and advice.

While the simplest way of providing for someone may be to bequeath money and assets to them directly, this may not be the most *efficient* way of providing for them. There is a risk that if the person receives too much they may lose valuable state benefits such as disability allowance. Also, those with a learning disability or mental illness may have to be made wards of court should it be judged that they are incapable of managing their own affairs.

You may therefore consider establishing a discretionary trust during your lifetime or in your will. This allocates assets assigned to be used for the beneficiary's benefit. The trustees have absolute discretion over how the trust fund is managed, and not the person for whom the trust is established. You must therefore make sure that you pick only people you trust as trustees and this ensures that no one can financially exploit the disabled person.

A discretionary trust gives the trustees power to invest the capital and use the interest from the investment for the beneficiary. You can set rules governing the trust which exclude trustees giving capital to the individual – to avoid interfering with the person's state benefits, for example. The trust may give money to pay for services directly or through a service provider.

You should also look at how the funds will be distributed after the beneficiary's death. You should get specialist advice on how to do this. There is a benefit in giving the funds for the individual's life only. Trust funds are taxed at an initial rate of 6 percent and subsequently at an annual rate of 1 percent. However, trusts established for people suffering from disabilities are, subject to Revenue approval, tax free.

You should consult all of those involved – including the trustees – before making any decision. Talk to relatives and other children you may have and explain what you intend to do. You should also consult a solicitor to explore your options. And, as with all of the advice to date – do it early.

12

Your Golden Years

We face different challenges as we age. Some of us will be fortunate; we may pass through our later years without illness or discomfort and die comfortably, in as pleasant a way as possible.

Taking good care of your health before you retire will help to improve your health in your later years. A good diet, physical and mental exercise and a positive outlook can all contribute to general wellbeing in later years. Building up a social network helps to maintain good health, too; community and active aged groups play an important role in this. However, planning for your own care should you become ill is a good precaution.

Illness is an unfortunate reality and tends to affect us more as we age. There is supposed to be free health care available for everyone in Ireland. However, the reality is that in many cases you may have to pay for this 'free' service. For example, you currently have to pay a fee of €100 if you attend an accident and emergency/casualty service without a referral from your general practitioner. Those with medical cards and some other groups are exempt from this charge. There are also in-patient, prescription and other charges for those who don't qualify for an exemption.

Recent trends and statements of intent by politicians suggest that future governments will increase and levy more charges for health services. This means that those planning their retirement need to seriously consider alternative ways of providing for their health-care in their later years.

Private health insurance is an obvious alternative. There is now competition in the Irish health insurance market, but the newer companies tend to target younger, more profitable customers. At present, there is confusion about the long-term survival of the government's approach of community rating and risk equalisation, which aimed to ensure that customers would not be discriminated against on the basis of their age or medical condition. This was challenged in the courts and has been replaced with a tax relief system and a community rating levy which aim to achieve the same outcome as the previous risk equalisation approach. The tax and levy arrangements may be no more than a temporary stopgap measure. The government intends to support this initiative with another which would encourage people to take out health insurance at an earlier age so that there are sufficient younger members in insurance schemes to support the older ones.

Commentators suggest that the cost of health insurance for the elderly will increase substantially in the future. Already, insurance companies are increasing their charges to cover procedures which are mainly used by older people.

All of this suggests that people will have to pay substantially more for their health insurance as they grow older. You will need to take this into account when planning the funding of your later years. Government policy will determine just how much you will have to pay, but it would be naive to assume that community rating will survive in its present form. Therefore, you'll need to provide for this potentially substantial extra cost.

The government has introduced a means test for a medical card for the over-seventies. You are allowed a means of €700 a week (gross) for a single person and twice that for a couple; you may qualify even if your income is above this and where there is a case of hardship. The card entitles you to a range of medical services for free or relatively little. There is now a charge for prescriptions, too: the Drugs Payment Scheme means that you only have to pay a maximum of €120 for prescribed medicines.

Living with incapacity

This book has emphasised that you should look at your home should you ever redevelop it and identify whether you could continue to live in it if you were to become physically incapacitated. There are simple changes, such as the addition of a wheelchair ramp, adding a downstairs bedroom etc, that can be of great value if you became disabled in your later years.

Local authorities provide grants to help older people adapt their houses so that they can continue living in them after an accident or the onset of an illness. Called the Mobility Aids Grants Scheme, these grants are means tested and households only qualify if they have a household income of less than €30,000. Older people can also avail of a Housing Adaptation Grant for people with disabilities, although you cannot apply for both grants. Your local authority administers these grants.

Local authorities sometimes provide special accommodation for older people living in their area. This is usually in group or community accommodation, often with wardens and special alarms. Certain voluntary bodies also provide similar accommodation for older people. These are usually charitable bodies and charges are based on what individuals can afford to pay. There are also some private developments which have been established for older communities. These are commercial operations and you must pay to reside in them at normal commercial rates, either as an owner-occupier or through renting.

Local authority, voluntary and commercial residences are for the older generally, rather than for specifically those who are incapacitated. They are usually adapted to meet frailer older people's needs. There is a shortage of such accommodation and there are often waiting lists for places in them.

Care in your home

Those who are or become incapacitated may need help to continue living in their own home. The HSE may provide help through the Community Care Services in the form of home help or through a public health nurse. All medical card holders are entitled to these services.

The HSE Home Care Services are provided in different ways depending upon your region. In some cases they provide these directly, while in others these services are provided through voluntary or other bodies. They may also provide a grant towards the employment of a private carer.

People who need to be cared for in their home may be entitled to a range of payments such as an allowance for a carer, a carer's benefit, respite grant and a mobility grant. All of these are aimed at helping you continue living in your own home or independently in specially-designed accommodation.

Nursing home care

Up until recently, some people received nursing home care in a public nursing home without charge; those in privately-run nursing homes had to pay the entire cost of their care. Those paying for their nursing home care had to do so from their own resources or had to have it paid for them by family. This was seen as inequitable and a new 'Fair Deal' was introduced to rectify this.

Under the Fair Deal, a person who is clinically assessed and found to require nursing home care only has to pay 80 percent of their pension income for that care. (A spouse living at home will receive 50 percent of the joint income.) The HSE pays the remainder. In return, the HSE is entitled to take up to 15 percent of the value of the person's assets at a rate of 5 percent per annum for the first three years. This is effectively a loan that the HSE gives to the recipient and it takes what is the equivalent of a mortgage on the person's assets. This is not collected until the person's assets are disposed of after his or her death.

You must choose to live in a nursing home (public or private) that the HSE has approved for this scheme. The funding for it is limited, so it isn't guaranteed that everyone will be accepted immediately or at all. You should note too that a government think tank has recommended that the amount the HSE's percentage takes of a person's assets should be increased from 15 to 20 percent. Those planning for their future care should recognise that it's likely that the government will continue to increase the amount that it takes in the future. You may need to transfer part of your assets to your next of kin well before you need nursing home care in order to reduce the potential outgoings that you will have to pay.

You may need to provide for:

- additional healthcare costs if you don't have insurance

- taxis if you can no longer drive and don't have access to public transportation

- modifying your home

- hiring home help

- paying for special accommodation

- nursing home care.

And in the end . . .

There is only one certainty in life, and that's death. It may not be a pleasant thought, but you should think about providing for your funeral and any other activity you may want to mark your passing.

One of the many charges that your estate will face will include buying a burial plot – if you choose to be buried rather than cremated. A plot in a cemetery can cost up to €2,500, and there are additional charges for actually opening it for a burial (these can amount to €750). Coffins are expensive and may reach €2,500 for a high quality one, and a funeral home will charge between €2,000 and €8,000. Then, you may wish to have a singer or a group perform at your service: churches will expect donations and other venues will charge for their use. You may want to give the guests at your funeral some food and drinks, and you will have to pay for this too. Your headstone and grave maintenance will account for a further few thousand euro, depending on your wishes.

If you wish to leave sufficient funds for your send-off, you must make provisions early. You can take out a life policy to cover these costs, but using savings may be a better way of covering these needs. Presuming that you plan to live to a great age, then paying for a life assurance policy in your later years will prove to be expensive. You are best to have built up a fund prior to your retirement.

Useful Web Sites and Further Information

Active Retirement Ireland is the largest national network of local and voluntary groups in Ireland.

www.activeirl.ie

The Citizens' Information Board provides details on all aspects of the Public Services and citizens' entitlements.

www.citizensinformation.ie

The Department of Enterprise Trade and Employment's website gives guidance on starting your own business

www.entemp.ie

The HSE is responsible for providing healthcare services in Ireland.

www.hse.ie

The Money Advice and Budgeting Service (Ireland) is a free national, confidential and independent service for people in debt or at risk of getting into it.

www.mabs.ie

The website of **Age and Opportunity** gives a list of contacts for those promoting the greater participation in society of older people.

www.olderinireland.ie

The Pensions Board regulates occupational pensions schemes and provides detailed advice on pensions and pension provision.

www.pensionsboard.ie

The Revenue's website gives information on all aspects of taxation in Ireland.

www.revenue.ie

A guide to all of the steps involved in starting your own business.

www.startingyourownbusinessinireland.ie

The official website of the **Department of Social and Family Affairs** contains useful information and many of their forms and documentation available for download.

www.welfare.ie

For more information on the numerous and often complicated aspects of successfully planning your inheritance and succession, see *Inheritance and Succession: The Complete Irish Guide* by John G. Murphy and Jason Dunne.

And for a handy guide to making your will, see Murphy and Dunne's expert *Make Your Will: The Irish Guide to Putting Your Affairs in Order* for a calm and clear approach to the process.

For further information on some of the tax reliefs discussed in this book, from work- and property/housing-related reliefs to reliefs for medical expenses, see Aidan Kelly's useful guide to the maze of allowances, rates, credits and bands, *Get Your Tax Back! The Irish Guide to Unlocking Your Allowances*.